DICKINSON MIDDLE SCHOOL LIBRARY

Golf Techniques: How to Improve Your Game

Golf Techniques:
How to Improve Your Game

Parker Smith

Photographs by Meryl Joseph
Illustrations by Dom Lupo

FRANKLIN WATTS | NEW YORK | LONDON

Cover by Seymour Schlatner

Library of Congress Cataloging in Publication Data

Smith, Parker.
   Golf techniques.

   (A Concise guide)
   SUMMARY: Includes information on equipment, essential techniques, and a glossary of golfing terms.
   1. Golf–Juvenile literature. [1. Golf] I. Title.
GV965.S655   796.352   73-3048
ISBN 0-531-02627-2

Copyright © 1973 by Parker Smith
Printed in the United States of America
6 5 4 3

Contents

Introduction *1*
Section One: How to Buy a Set of Clubs
A Word About Clubs *2*
Section Two: The Four Essentials
The Grip *6*
The Stance *13*
Alignment *18*
The Swing *22*
Section Three: Tips on Trouble Shots
Uneven Lies *32*
In the Sand *37*
Section Four: Putting
How to Read a Green *42*
Stance and Stroke *46*
Section Five: The Proper State of Mind
Relaxation *51*
Glossary *56*
Bibliography *59*
Index *61*

*To Jean, Sheila,
three typewriters
and John...
We can make it happen*

Golf Techniques: How to Improve Your Game

Introduction

This book is written as a guide to understanding the logic of golf, with an emphasis on fundamentals. The material in this book applies to those who have never played, as well as to those who play the tour. All good golf shots follow logical laws; all mistakes are fundamental lapses. If you believe this and have the presence of mind to remember these laws when you're trying to hit the ball, you'll score far beyond (I should say below) your physical capability.

PARKER SMITH
Brooklyn, New York

Section One: How to Buy a Set of Clubs

A Word About Clubs

A beginner's set of golf clubs generally consists of a driver (1-wood), 3-wood, 3-iron, 5-iron, 7-iron, 9-iron, and putter. This gives the newcomer a club to handle every type of shot he's likely to encounter on the course except for the sand trap. The 9-iron is just not suited to trap play around the green, and the beginner will invariably spend a good part of the day playing in the sandboxes. A beginner should therefore also have a sand wedge, too. It could change his whole attitude about the game and speed up his learning process.

It is an important day in the life of the beginner when he realizes his shot is a little too far for his 9-iron, yet he knows he'll go over the green with his 7-iron. At this point, he's ready to get an 8-iron. Many people realistically never achieve that day. But many eventually get around to buying a matched set of fourteen clubs just in case they happen to hit the shot correctly.

The theoretical difference in each club is ten yards. This difference arises from slight changes in club length and face loft. The ten-yard figure works well when the balls are hit by a machine but varies with each individual who swings a club. Unfortunately, the average player rarely has a set of clubs that are best suited to him. He usually buys clubs according to brand name, player endorsement, advertisements, or appearance. Price, which would logically be a major factor in club selection, is often a minor consideration.

Even further down on the list of criteria used in buying clubs is usefulness (which should of course be at the top). The club could be the wrong swing weight, have the wrong shaft flex, and be entirely too long. But into the bag it goes if it is an impressive brand, looks good, or "feels" right when the golfer takes two practice swings in the department store.

How to Shop for a Set of Clubs

Go to a golf pro and have him watch you hit a couple of buckets of balls on different days. Tell him what your usual problems are (hooking, slicing, or even hitting it fat, that is, hitting the ground behind the ball). Then have him suggest a type of club that's designed to help you correct your problems. Ask him if you can take the driver, the 5-iron, and the 9-iron from the set out to the range and hit a couple of buckets in front of him. The cost of the set is immaterial; it must help your game to be worth anything. This doesn't mean that you're going to wind up with an inexpensive set of clubs, however, for the more expensive sets are obviously better made and are thus more likely to be beneficial to your game.

How to Suit a Set to Your Game

The type of club you can handle depends on your build, your coordination, your dedication, and your ability, more or less in that order. It may seem obvious to say that girls need lighter clubs, whereas strong, athletic types can use heavier ones. But you'll often see the opposite—for absolutely no reason.

Here are some general guidelines to follow in buying clubs. Never swing a club that's too heavy for you, but don't be afraid to try one that's too light. The lighter club can be swung faster and give you more clubhead speed in the crucial impact area. If you choose a club that's lighter than you've been using, you

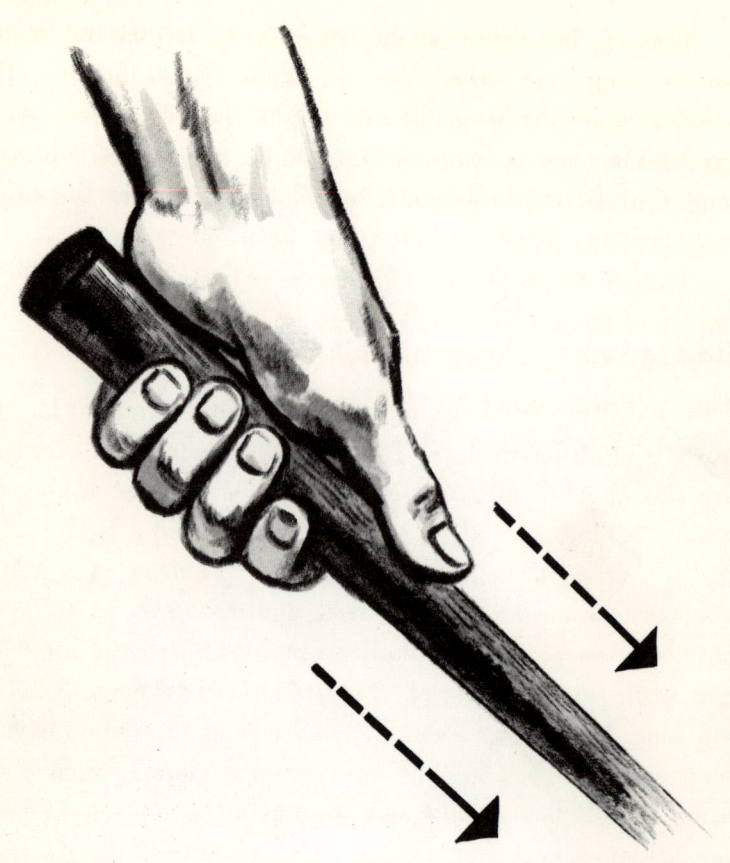

Hold the club at the very top, then slide your hand down the shaft until your fingertips rest against the pad of your thumb. This will give you your ideal grip size.

---

might try a stiffer shaft at the same time to help control the tendency you'll have toward wildness. A stiff shaft will hit the ball straighter because it can't be bent as much. But only strong, supple people should combine stiff shafts and heavier swing weights.

The tall, thin golfer should shop in the D-2 to D-4 swing-weight range and should use stiff shafts if he's athletic. The heavyset player is better off with D-0 to D-3, depending on his hand action, and he shouldn't use a stiff shaft unless he hits a long, wild ball. Girls should shop in the C-8 to D-1 swing-weight range and buy regular shafts.

To find the proper grip size for your hand, hold a driver at the top of the grip in your left hand. Slide your hand down the grip until the tips of the fingers rest firmly against the thumb. This is the right grip thickness for you.

Section Two: The Four Essentials

The Grip

A good grip is the foundation of the golf swing. When you consider that the hands are the only part of your body that touch the club, you can see that it is crucial that they be placed in such a way as to afford maximum control of the club's path. The right-handed grip actually favors the left hand, but for good reason. The left hand is in control of the club for two-thirds of the golf swing. It must be the intelligent guide and master of the stronger right hand until the precise moment of impact with the ball. At address, it is the left side of the body that is closest to the target. In order for the hands and club to be moving toward the target as the club accelerates toward impact, the left side of the body must lead the right side into the proper position.

To ensure this left-side dominance, the grip is designed so that two knuckles are visible on the left hand and only one is visible on the right, that of the thumb. The left hand is turned so that the V formed by the left thumb and forefinger point to the right shoulder. The V of the right hand also points to the right shoulder, again giving strength to the left hand on the grip. This permits the left hand to control the backswing and downswing, allowing the physically stronger right hand to take over only as the hands roll through the impact zone.

Since the hands are the only connection you have with the club, you must grip the club lightly enough to feel the weight of the clubhead as it swings. This frees your body from tension and keeps your hands active so they can supply control and power.

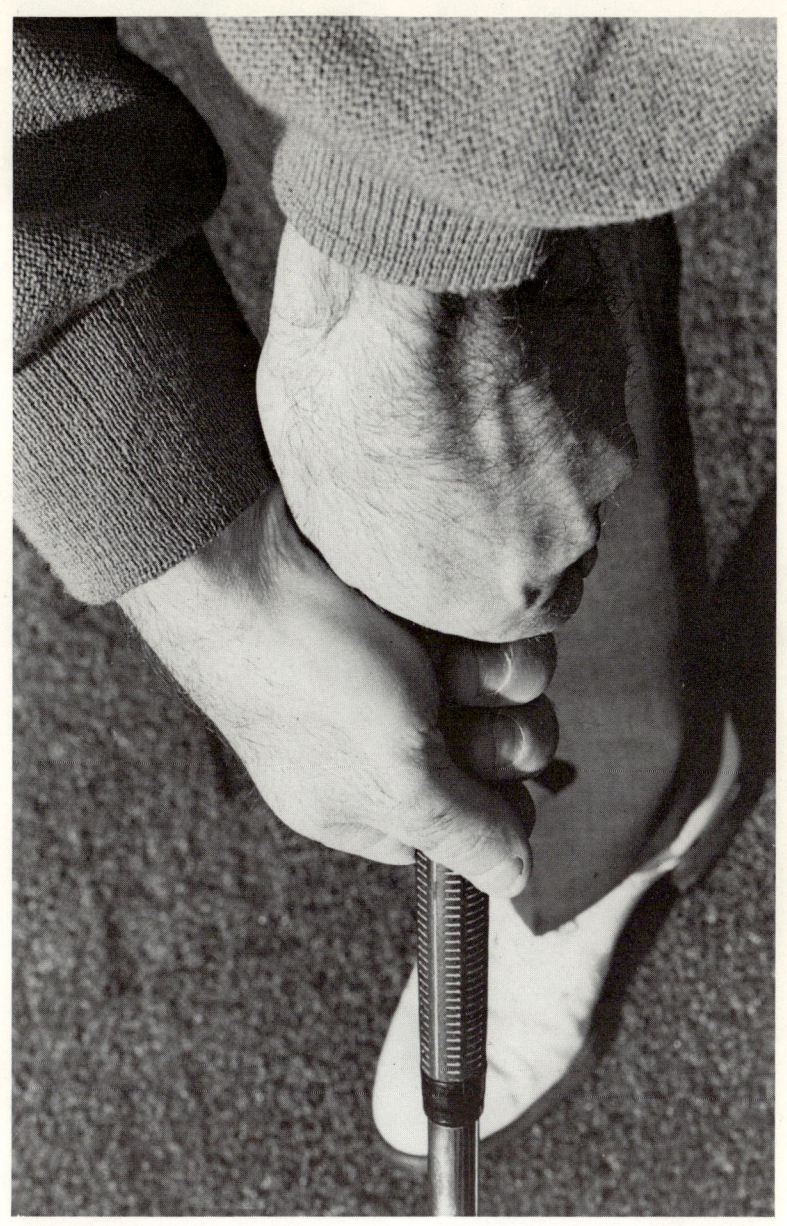

The Grip: Two knuckles showing on left hand, "V's" pointing at right shoulder.

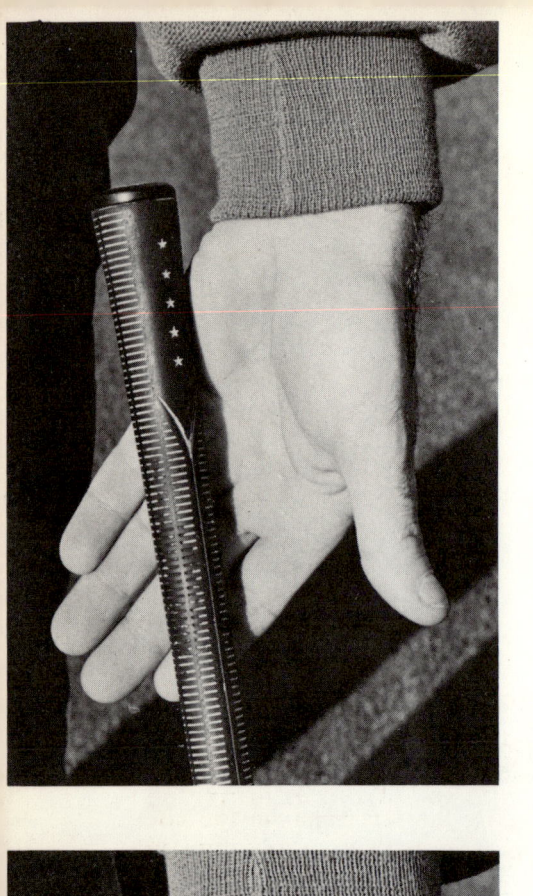
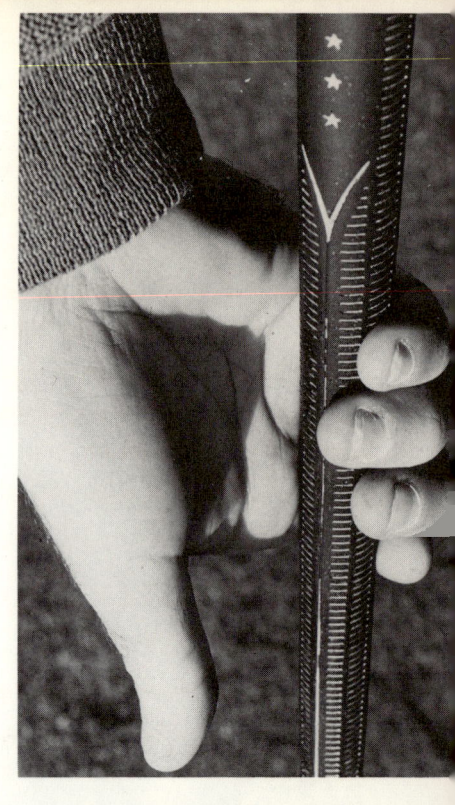
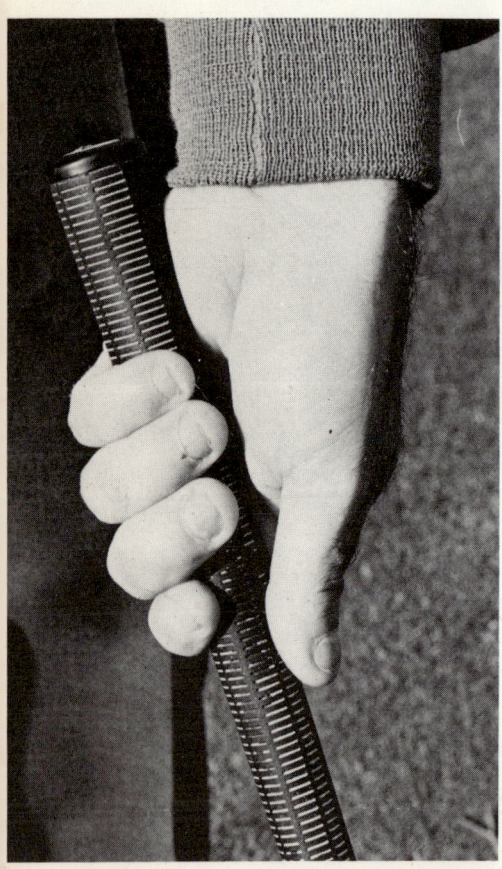
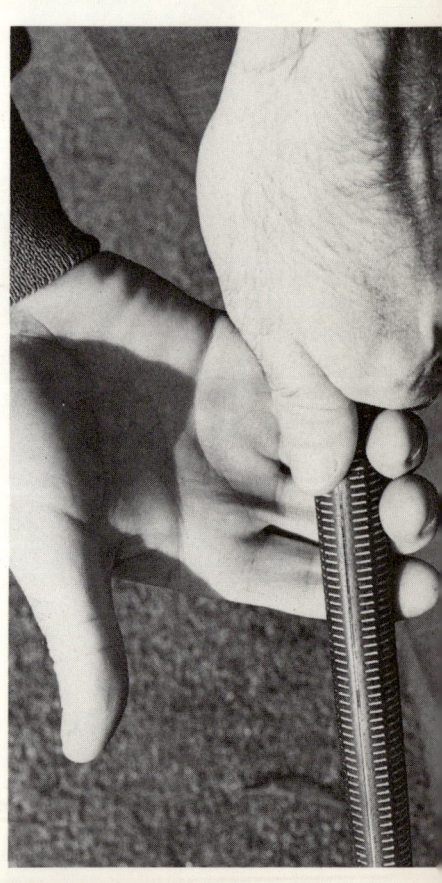

If you're an advanced player, or one who plays frequently, it is wise to check your grip at least once on every hole just to make sure that no errors are creeping in because of carelessness. The top player will check his grip before every shot even though he's hit so many balls his hands are practically molded to the club. The reason for this is clear—a bad grip is a bad shot.

If you're a beginner, master the grip and keep it free of tension and you're well on your way to becoming a good player.

The three basic grips are the Vardon, the interlock, and the ten-finger, or baseball, grip.

The Vardon Grip

The Vardon, or overlapping, grip is used by the vast majority of golfers. It suits itself to almost any size hand and unifies the hands on the club without forcing pressure on any of the fingers. To form this grip, start by placing the left hand on the club about a quarter of an inch from the top. Rest the club diagonally across the ends of the fingers as shown and then close the last three fingers firmly around the grip. Then close the thumb and forefinger so that the left thumb is slightly to the right of center. The right hand is placed on the club by extending it in the same way you would to shake hands with someone you're not so happy about meeting. Grip with the fingers, but don't try to squeeze. The palm of the right hand swallows the left thumb, and the little finger of the right hand is then placed in the crook of the first and second fingers of the left. Check to make sure that the V's

(Above Left) The club lies diagonally across the fingers of the left hand.
(Above Right) The club is then grasped firmly by the last three fingers.
(Below Left) The hand then closes around the grip, with the thumb going just to the right of center.
(Below Right) The club is gripped with the fingers of the right hand.

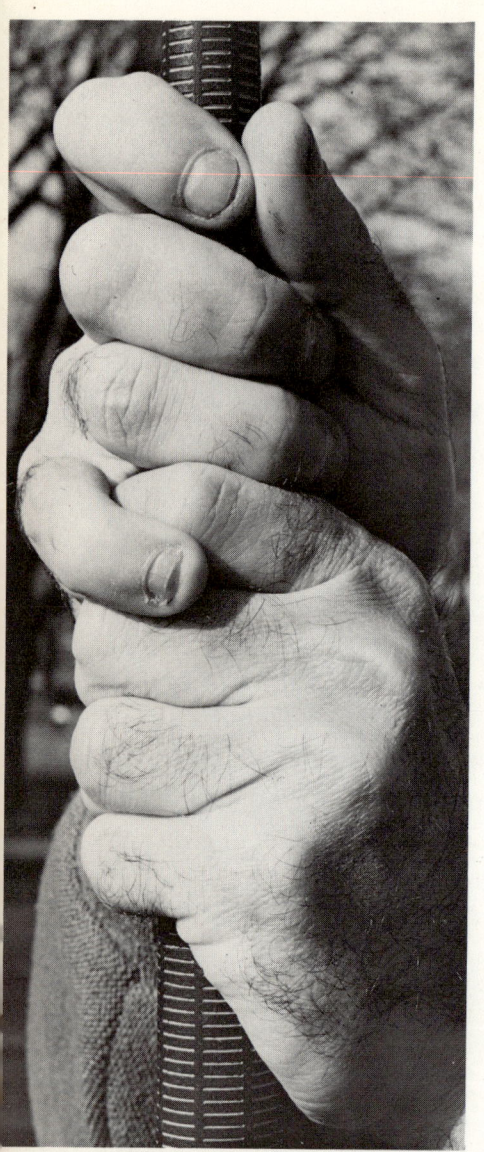 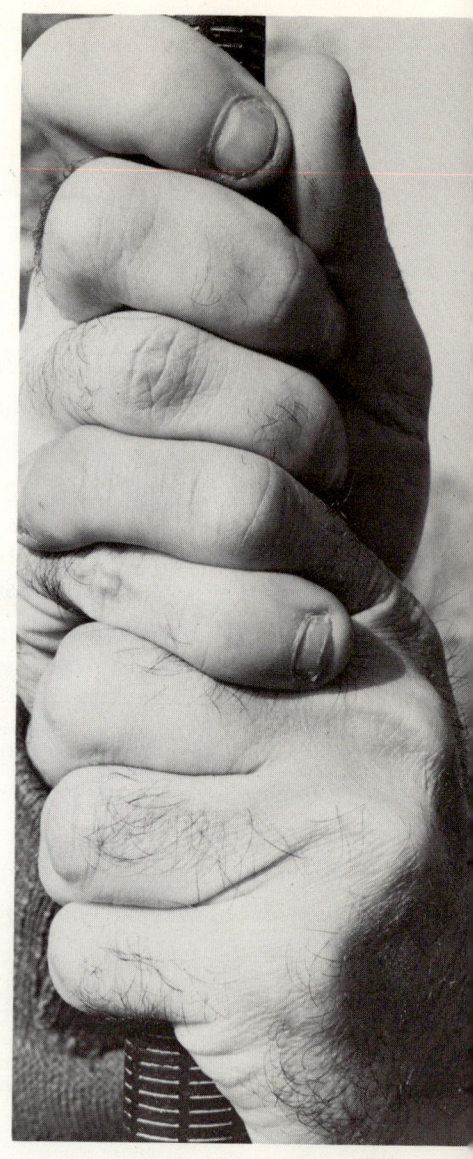

(Left) The completed Vardon Grip: The pinky of the right hand is draped in the crease formed by the first two fingers of the left hand.
(Right) The Interlocking Grip: The pinky of the right hand and the forefinger of the left wrap around each other.

formed by the thumb and forefingers of both hands point to your right shoulder. This gives the desired favoritism to the left hand, which must remain in control of the swing.

The Interlocking Grip

The interlocking grip is achieved the same way as the Vardon grip with one exception. Instead of placing the little finger of the right hand in the crook of the first two fingers of the left hand, it is interlocked with the first finger of the left hand. This is an especially useful grip for people with small fingers who might feel strain trying to hold the right pinky in the crook. This grip unifies the hands and feels more natural than the Vardon grip, and is the one used by Jack Nicklaus. The interlocking grip will feel good almost immediately and can be used without any fear of regret. It has often been maligned as a "hooker's grip" because it supposedly makes it easier to roll the right hand at impact, but those rumors were probably not started by someone with smallish fingers.

The Ten-Finger Grip

Here again, the same basic principles of facing palms and V's pointing at the right shoulder apply. The ten-finger grip differs from the others only in what the pinky does on the right hand. Instead of overlapping or interlocking, it just grabs the club and tells the first finger of the left hand to move down on the grip a little. If you're an ex-Little Leaguer, this grip will probably feel the most natural of all, as it is similar to the way a baseball bat is gripped. But you should fight the tendency to use this grip unless your hands are very small and the grip on your club is too thick. The golf swing depends too much on complete control to use a grip that fails to unify the hands. You will be way ahead

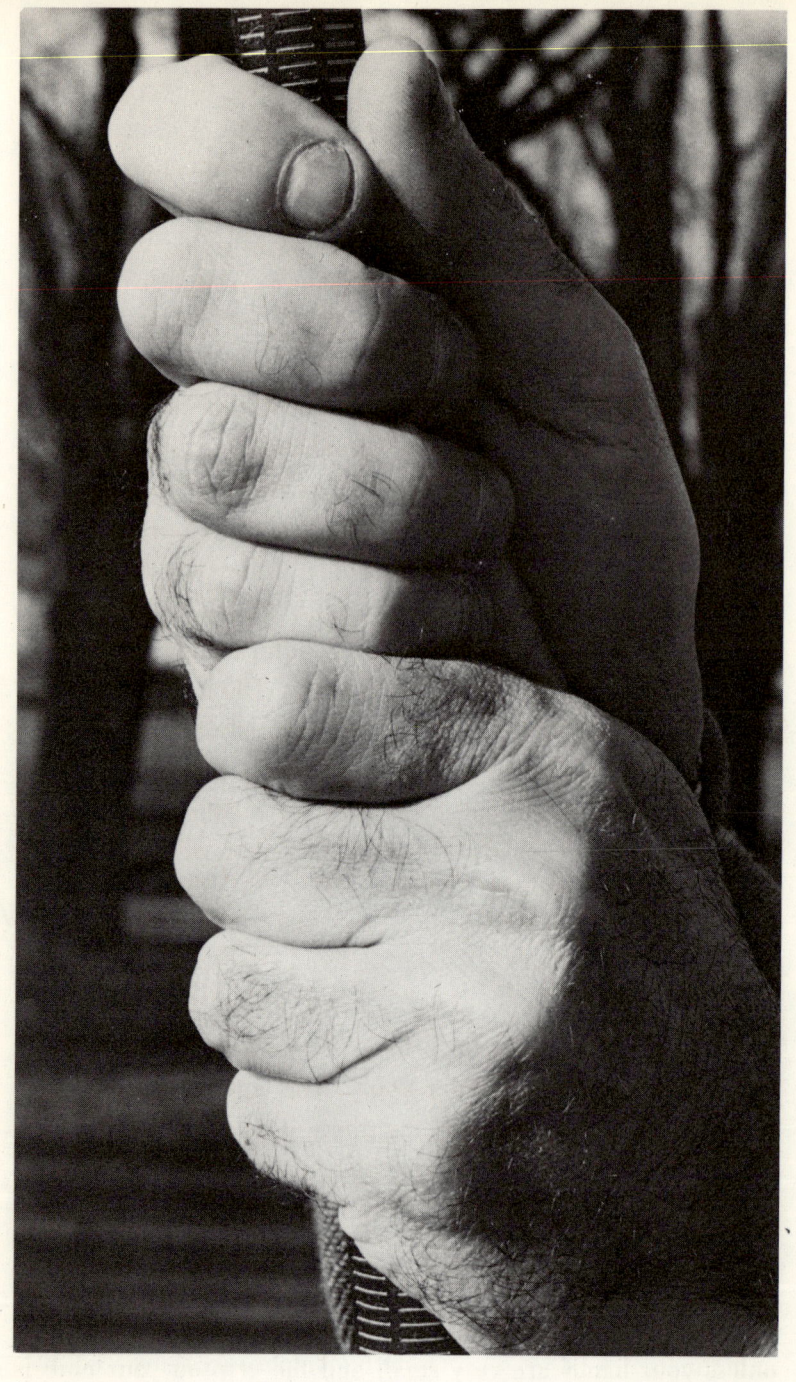

The Ten-Finger Grip: All ten fingers are in contact with the club's grip.

of the game if you learn to use the Vardon or interlocking grip, because they're designed to get the hands to work together.

If you're still unsure about the left-hand grip, stand a few feet away from someone and have him toss the club to you with the club vertical and the grip at the bottom. Catch the grip in your left hand, and see if you don't catch it with the left hand in almost precisely the same position as has been prescribed.

As you will see, golf is a very natural and very logical game.

The Stance

The stance, the second of the four essentials, is the least complicated. In your most casual, confident manner, stand up. If you're comfortable, look at your feet. How far apart are they—shoulder width? Look at your toes. Are they pointed slightly outward? Are your knees slightly flexed? All you have to do is put down the book and pick up a club. Push your knees out about an inch and bend slightly from the waist, and you've got a perfect stance. The secret is simply to be as relaxed standing over a golf ball as you are waiting for a bus. Be natural, be comfortable. The stance should only vary for special shots or special physiques.

The Square Stance

The square stance is precisely what was just described. The term *square* is derived from the relationship that the feet establish with the ball. A better term might be the *parallel* stance, because this is what it really is. The feet are placed parallel to an imaginary line drawn from the target back through the ball, with the toes of both feet equidistant from that line. You can hit any kind of shot from this stance. It also affords you the best perspective of the relationship between the ball, the club, the target, and yourself.

The Open Stance

The open stance is taken by withdrawing the left foot back from the parallel lines that we have just described. This stance inhibits a full turn away from the ball because the body is already facing the target. Logically, then, the body must turn a few extra degrees in order to achieve a fully coiled position at the top of the backswing. It can therefore be especially beneficial to tall, thin players who have a tendency toward overly long backswings. A supple, thin body is thus corrected for its tendency to overturn. But a heavyset or muscular person merely compounds the lack of freedom already built into his swing.

The open stance makes it easier to hit a fade or a slice. The club has a tendency to follow the toe line. If you take an open stance, you'll more than likely cut across the ball from right-to-left. This presents a problem only when you're trying to hook the ball or when you get a little anxious and release your hands earlier than you should.

The Closed Stance

It does not necessarily follow that a closed stance will help you to hook if an open stance will help you to slice. It follows logically and physically, but there's a mental pitfall that catches all

Good golf posture is just a slight bend of the knees. The rest of the body remains in the same position it would assume when you stand up after sitting in a comfortable chair.

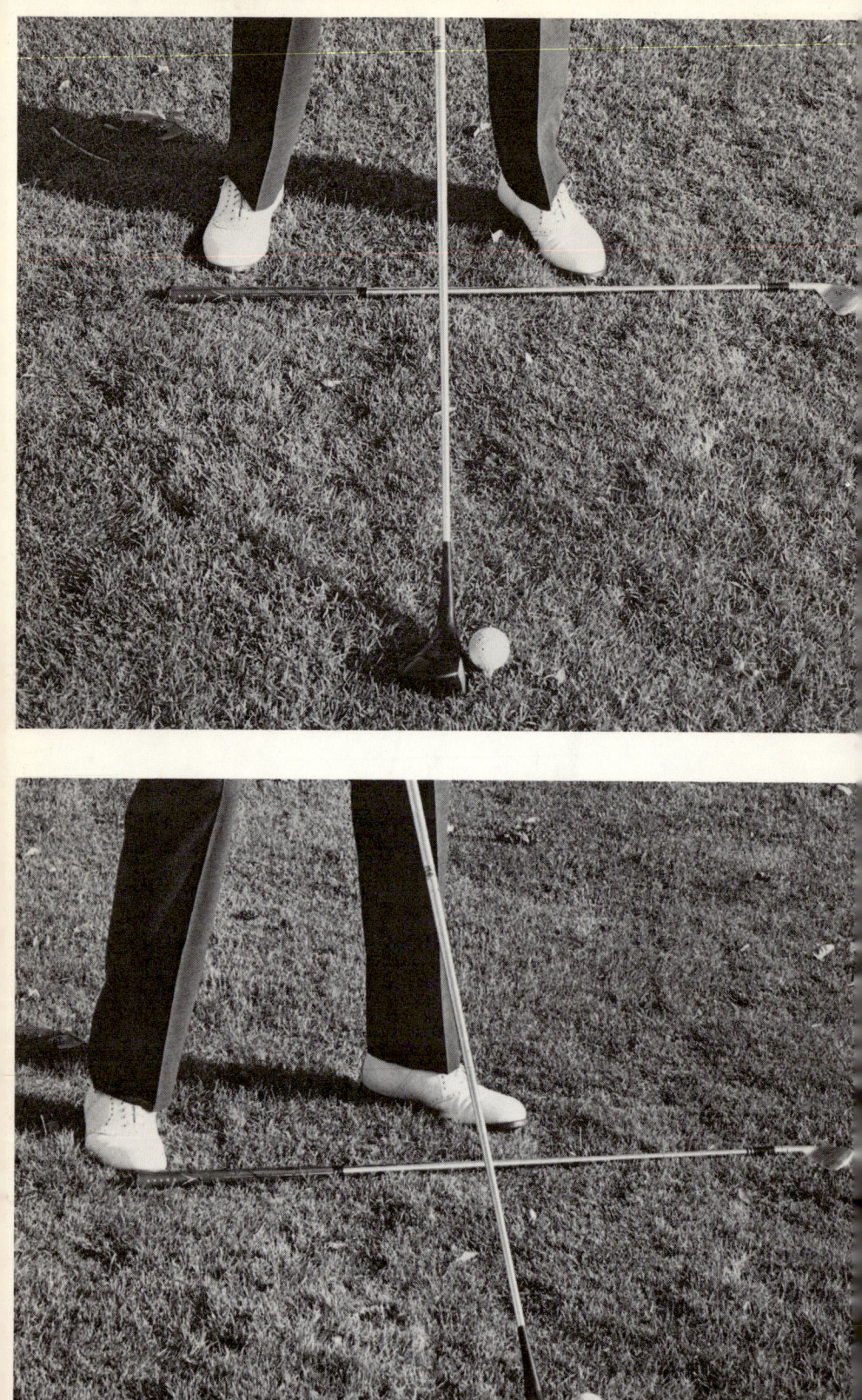

(Above Left) The Square Stance has the foot line parallel to the ball target line.

(Below Left) Open Stance: The left foot is withdrawn slightly from the parallel lines.

(Above) Closed Stance: The right foot is withdrawn from the parallel lines.

but the most aware. In the closed stance, the left foot is closer to the parallel line through the ball than the right foot. Therefore, your body is already slightly turned away from the target. This is ideal for the heavyset person who has trouble taking a full turn and is recommended for him . . . if he overcomes the pitfall.

When you close your stance, your view of the target is slightly changed. It seems to be behind you somewhere as you near impact on the downswing, so there is a definite tendency to go for the target instead of the ball. This pulls the club out of its natural collision course with the ball and you lose both speed and accuracy by shifting your aim in midswing. If you're going to close your stance, follow your toeline when you swing. The ball will then hook back into the target.

Alignment

A perfect swing that is improperly aimed is worthless or disastrous. On the other hand, if you're aligned correctly, all you need to think about is what you're doing with the club because a good swing will have to send the ball directly toward the target.

Techniques

There are two simple techniques or guidelines for alignment. The first is the use of a club as an aid. Whenever you practice, put a club on the ground parallel to the ball about twenty-eight inches away. This is the ideal distance for a person of average build, and if you take the trouble to use a yardstick, you'll discover that you'll feel most comfortable standing between twenty-six and thirty inches from the ball with your driver.

Once you've established your proper distance, take careful notice of the perspective you have of the hole from this position. Try to ingrain this perspective in your mind by drawing a mental line from the target to the ball.

Now leave the club lying on the ground and stand behind the ball. The ball will be directly on the target line, but the club that you used to set your stance will aim at a point about thirty feet to the left of the target. This is because the thirty-inch distance that you stand away from the ball is magnified as you look out into the distance.

You can get a good understanding of the relationship you

Using a club to ensure correct alignment. This should be a training aid to memorize perspective. You can't swing at the ball and have the club at your feet when you're on the golf course.

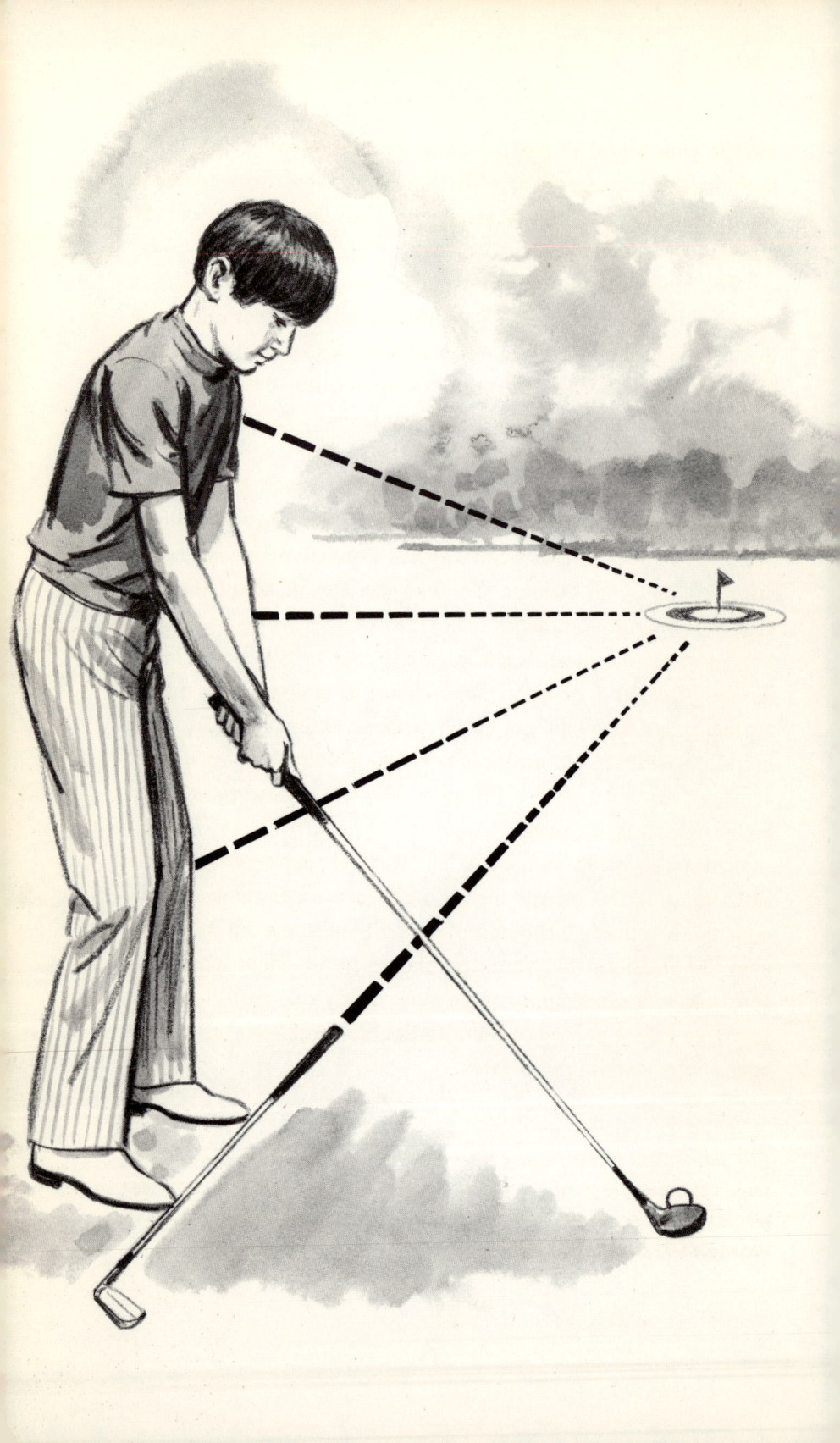

have to your target by realizing that the placement of your body to the left of your target at address is what allows your hands to swing the club freely away from your body and out toward the target during the downswing.

This first technique works excellently as a training device in practice. On the golf course, however, the rules do not allow you to swing with that club lying at your feet. You might not know, however, that the rules *do* permit you to place the club down while you assume your stance and require only that you remove it before you *actually* swing.

Rather than having to move the club after setting up on the course, try this second little trick to achieve correct alignment. Make use of nature. Every fairway has distinctive areas of coloration, foliage, and contour. You can use any or all of these as aids in lining up your shot.

Stand behind the ball and pick out your target. If you're on the tee of a par-4 or par-5 hole, choose a landing area that is realistic, one that you can reach without excessive effort. This helps to eliminate any desire to overswing and usually results in a longer shot than you've imagined because the swing is timed better when it isn't forced.

Once you've decided on a landing area, move your eyes a little left of the target and then bring them back to the tee. Draw a mental line thirty inches left of the ball and stake out with your eyes the positions that your feet should be in. Then look for a leaf, a tree, a sandtrap, or some other easily distinguishable object. Use it as a reference point to double-check your alignment once you're standing at address.

The entire torso forms parallel lines that come together at the target. The important thing to remember is to not position yourself in a way that would make lines cross (by excessively bending the knees or by tilting the shoulders too much).

The Swing

The Takeaway

The takeaway is made with the upper body acting as a unit. The left arm is kept straight and the club acts as an extension of the arm. The entire unit is moved in one piece by the left shoulder turning down and under the chin. The right hand and arm merely respond to the force generated by the left side.

This turning of the left shoulder will force the club away from the ball on a path that is slightly inside the imaginary line drawn from the target through the ball. You don't consciously have to guide the club inside this line; the left shoulder will do it for you. You must allow the club to leave the ground of its own accord once you've started it away from the ball. Don't pick it up or you're courting trouble. If you let the left shoulder do the work and hold the left arm and club as a straight unit, the club will lift from the ground at a point that is precisely the same distance from the ball as your hands are from the ground at address.

The Backswing

Once the club has left the ground, the outward and upward force will act upon your body as long as you don't tense up and prevent it. Tension will inhibit the natural acceleration and movement of the club. When the club reaches a point even with your waist, it will start to pull on your hips and force the right hip to turn away from the ball while the left hip reacts by going toward the ball. As the hips move, the left knee will also go out toward the ball. This will prevent an overshifting of weight to the right side and will eliminate any need for the left foot to be lifted, a

The Takeaway: The left shoulder, left arm, left hand, and club all move away from the ball as a unit. The club leaves the ground of its own accord, is NOT *lifted into the air by the hands.*

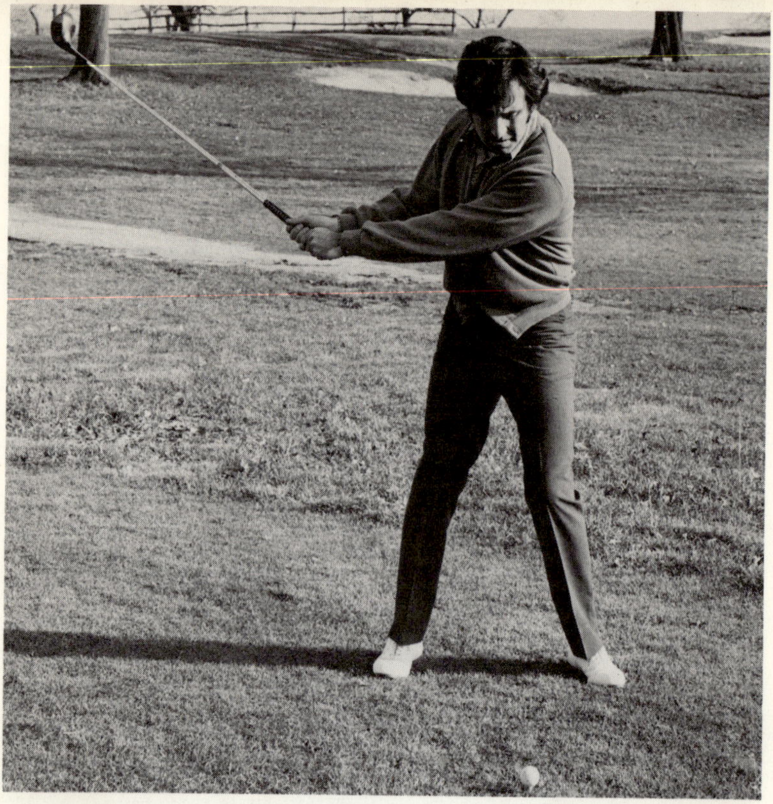

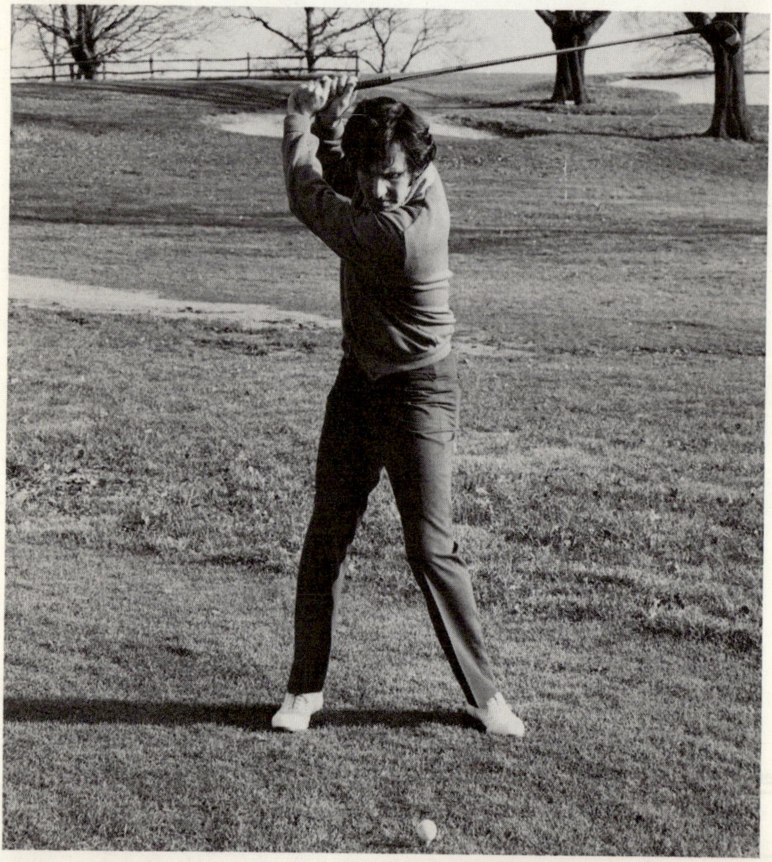

move that will almost surely throw your body off balance by forcing your weight to shift too rapidly.

The club will also take care of the cocking of your wrists as a result of centrifugal force. Once the club has passed the maximum extension point, it returns toward the body as it continues its ascent. This return puts the club behind the hands and pulls the wrists over into a cocked position at the top. All you have to do is stay relaxed enough to feel the weight of the club acting on your body, rather than get excited and try to have your body act on the club.

The Top of the Backswing

An examination of this position would show your left shoulder directly under your chin, your eyes on the ball, and your head in the same position as it was at address. Your upper chest is facing away from the hole, your left arm is straight, and your right arm is folded and next to your side. Your left knee points at the ball and your right leg is almost straight and supporting most of your weight. The club is horizontal in relation to the ground, and your wrists are fully cocked. This is the driver position. With the irons the club will probably not be horizontal because your arc is determined by the length of the shaft if you do everything correctly.

You've probably been made aware of the fact that you should pause at the top of the backswing. But try to imagine how

(Above) The Backswing: At this point the club starts to return toward the body, forcing the wrists to cock.

(Below) The Top of the Backswing: The important things to note are our pro's steady head, the balance his body demonstrates, and the fact that the left knee is turned to point at the back of the ball. Most beginners turn the knee too far and lose balance.

Key on the left thumb. By putting a little extra pressure on the left thumb at address, you'll be aware of it at the top of the backswing. When the thumb is flat and pointing at the target, your club is in the desired horizontal position.

long a pause you'd need to check out each of these points. You'd be there all day. The pause is nothing more than a natural delay that takes place as the club stops going up and back and starts coming down. To be sure you're in the right position at the top, you need only be aware of two things—your left thumb and your head. If your head hasn't moved and your left thumb is under the shaft, you're ready for the downswing. At address, put a little extra pressure on the grip with the left thumb. This way,

The Downswing: By initiating the downswing with a movement of the left hip, the left side is able to get out of the way by the time the right side moves into the impact area. Notice that the hands are still cocked.

you'll be aware of it at the top and you'll know immediately where the club shaft is.

The Downswing

Start the club back to the ball by sliding your left hip an inch or so to the left while simultaneously pulling down with the left hand. Once you've initiated the club's return to the ball, there is little left to do except feel its progress. The club will build up acceleration as it falls unless you tense up or try to alter its course. Since you started the action with your left side (which is only natural because the left side is closer to the target), the left side will remain in command until the club reaches the bottom of its arc.

Impact

Since that first movement of the left hip, your weight has slowly been shifting back over to your left side. When the club reaches the bottom of its arc, your left side will clear itself out of the way and let the right side take over as the club pulls it into and through the shot. At the exact bottom of the arc the club will brush the ground and move through the ball. The centrifugal force that cocked your wrists on the backswing will now uncock them and your stronger right hand will supply the punch to the shot.

The Follow-Through

If you've stayed relaxed, the club will still be accelerating for a few moments after impact, and the remainder of your weight will be pulled over onto the left side as the club swings through

---

Impact (just before): Look at the amount of snap that has occurred in the hands in the fraction of a second since the last picture. The club head is moving into the very bottom of its arc and the hands resemble the position they had at the very start of the swing.

Impact (just after): The club is accelerating after striking the ball and is now swinging out toward the target on the same low plane as it moved away from the ball on the takeaway. Observe the right knee and compare it in this photograph with the photographs before and after this one.

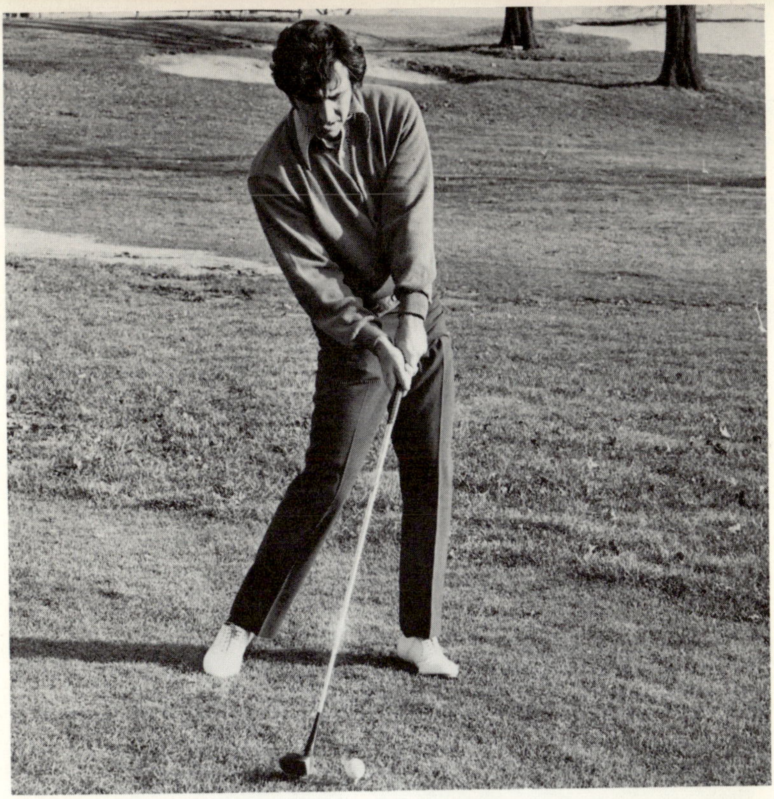

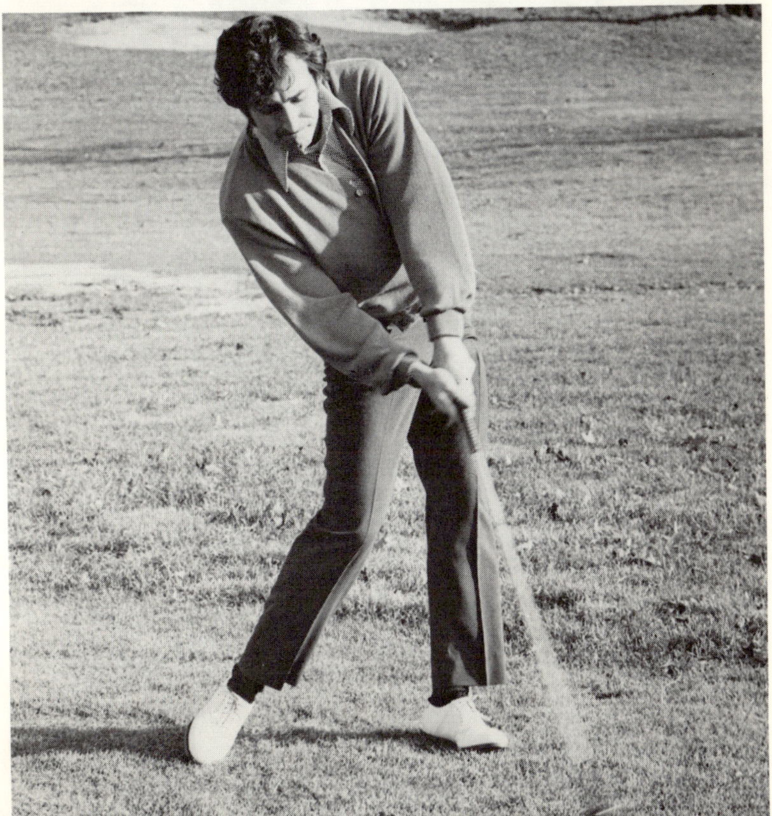

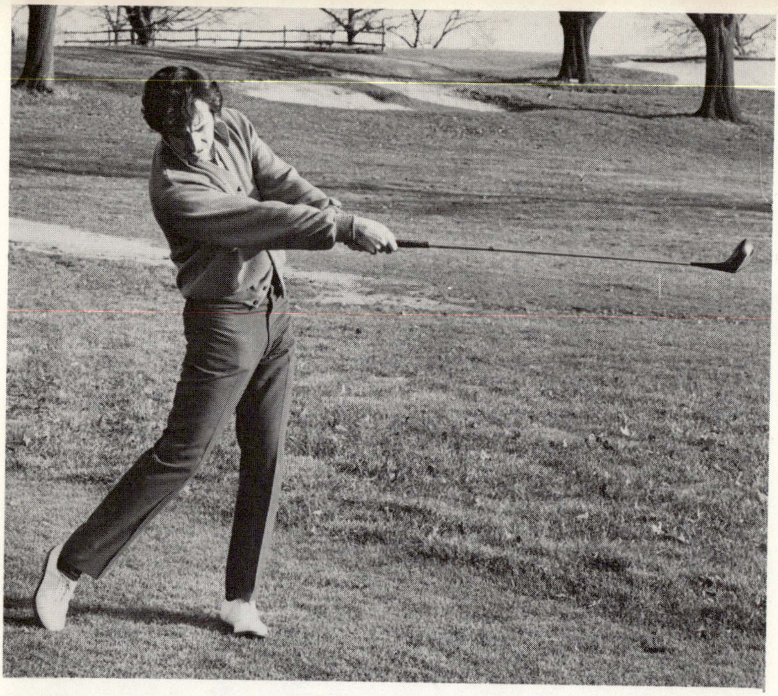

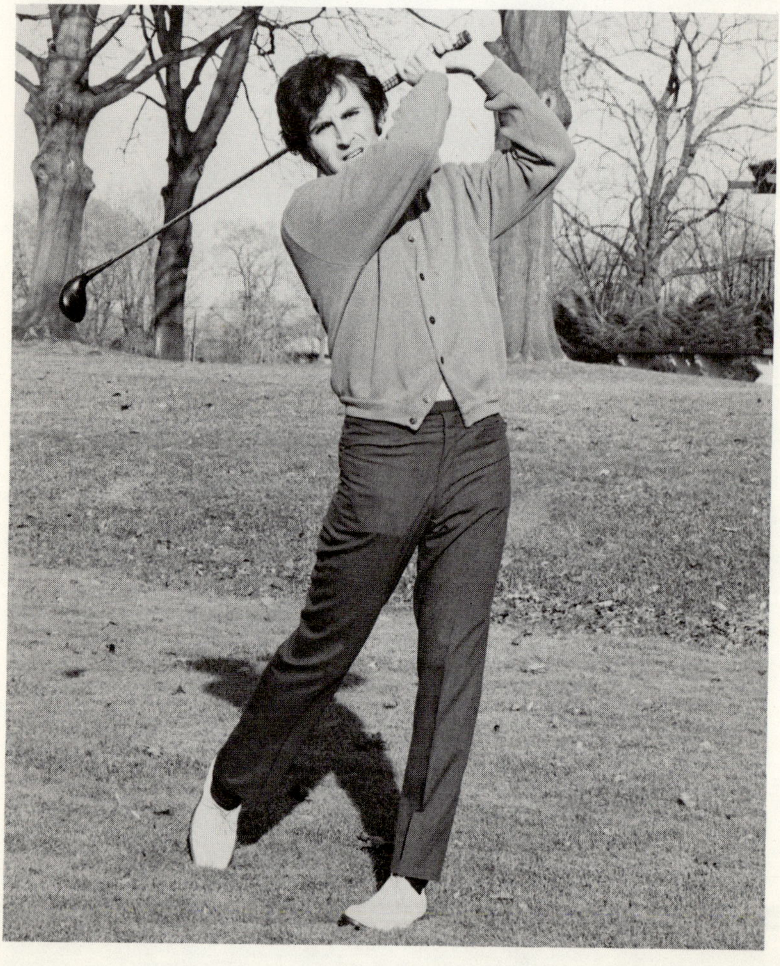

the ball and out toward the target. When the club is waist-high, both arms will be fully stretched just as they were at the same point in the backswing. When the club reaches its maximum extension point, it will return toward the body, pulling your hands into a high finish above your head.

The Follow-Through: The club's momentum coupled with the freedom of our pro's release has pulled his right knee and right arm out toward the target.

The Finish: Hands high (pulled there by the force of the club), weight balanced on the left leg (pulled there by the force of the club) and body facing the target (the club did that, too).

Section Three: Tips on Trouble Shots

Uneven Lies

Sidehill

The key to playing any uneven lie is the address position: *you must level yourself before you swing.*

On a sidehill lie where the ball is below the feet, stand closer to the ball, bend a little more from the waist, put your weight back on your heels and raise your hands slightly so that the club is soled, that is, its bottom is level with the ground. Each of these helps to compensate for the slope of the ground and all are natural movements you would make to balance yourself. Once you've assumed this position, take a normal swing and expect a fade equal to the slope of the ground. If the ground angle is twenty degrees, you should allow for a twenty-yard fade on a full shot.

If the ball is above your feet, set up with your weight forward of center. Stand a few inches farther away from the ball and balance on the balls of your feet. Choke down on the grip an inch and reach out to the ball to create a flatter arc. Again, try to position yourself so that the lie feels as though it is level. When you swing, follow the contour of the land just as you would for any other shot. Plan on a hook equal to the slope of the land.

Ball below feet: Upper body bent over, weight on heels to level you.

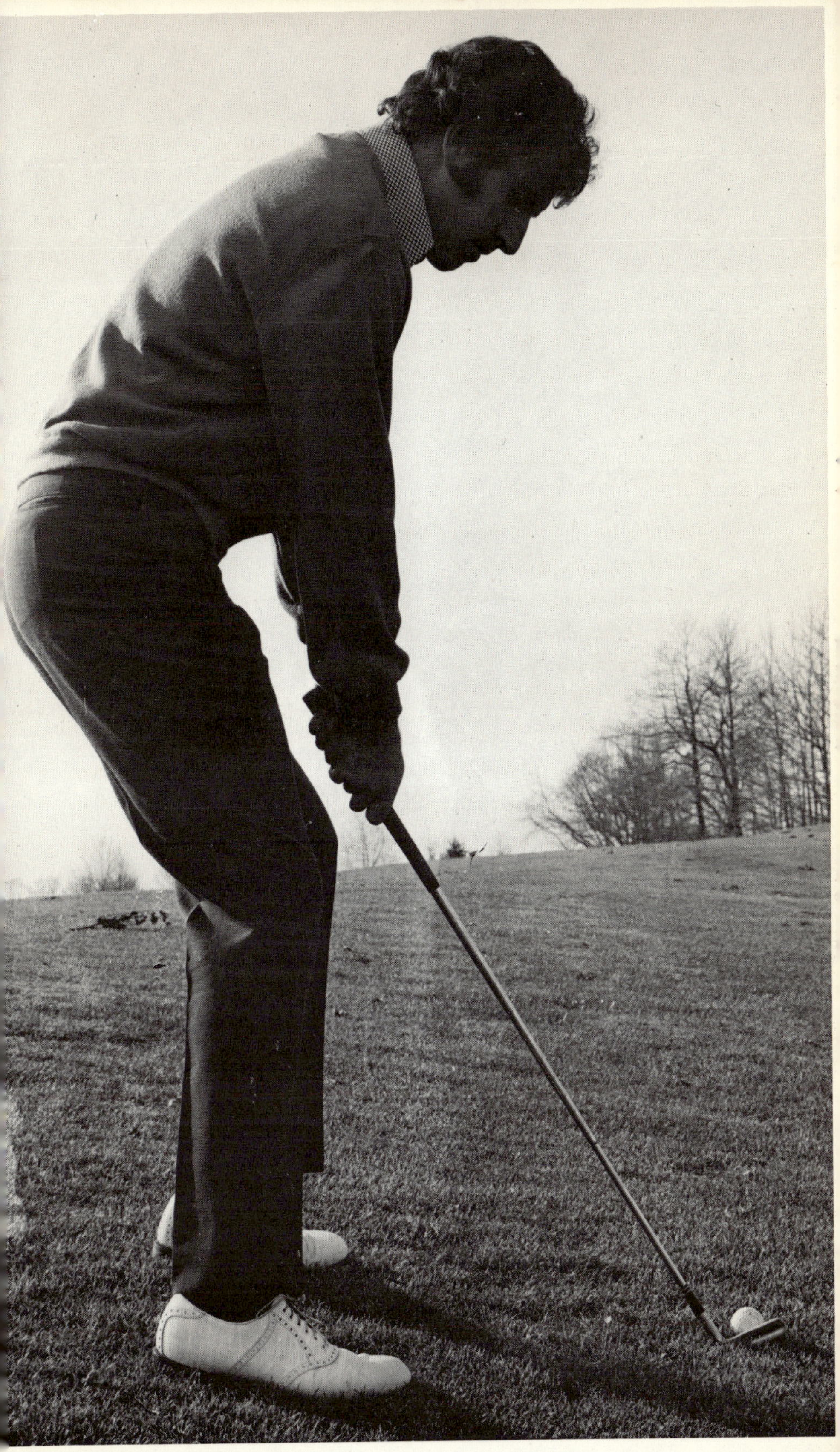

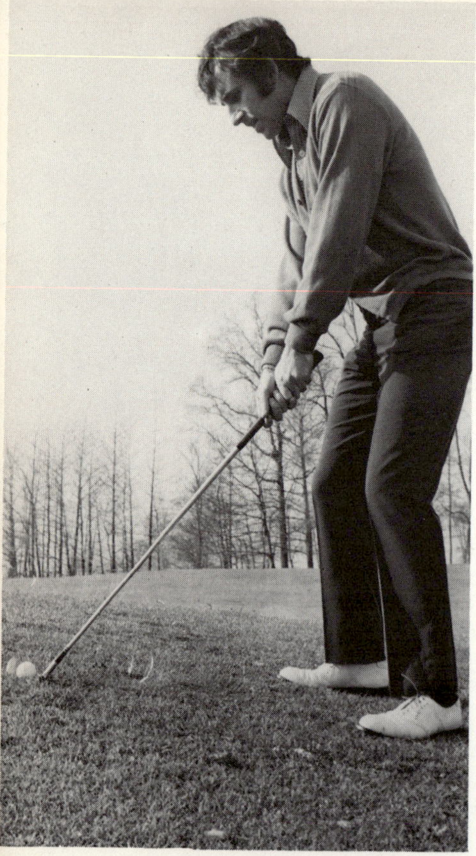

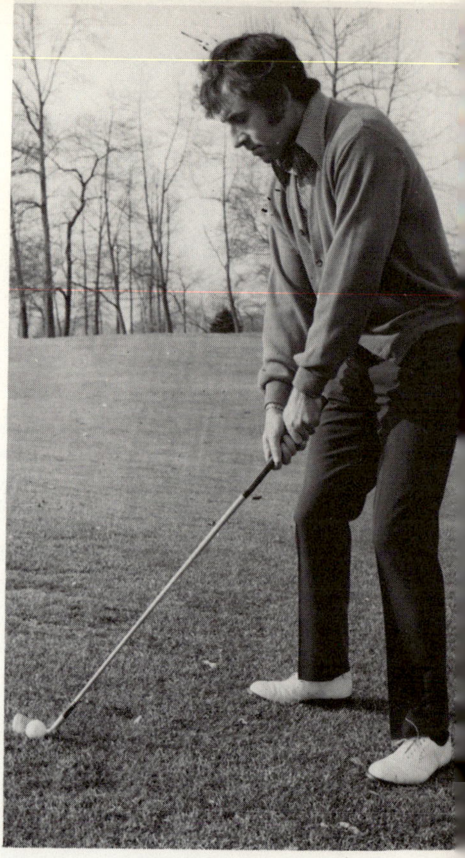

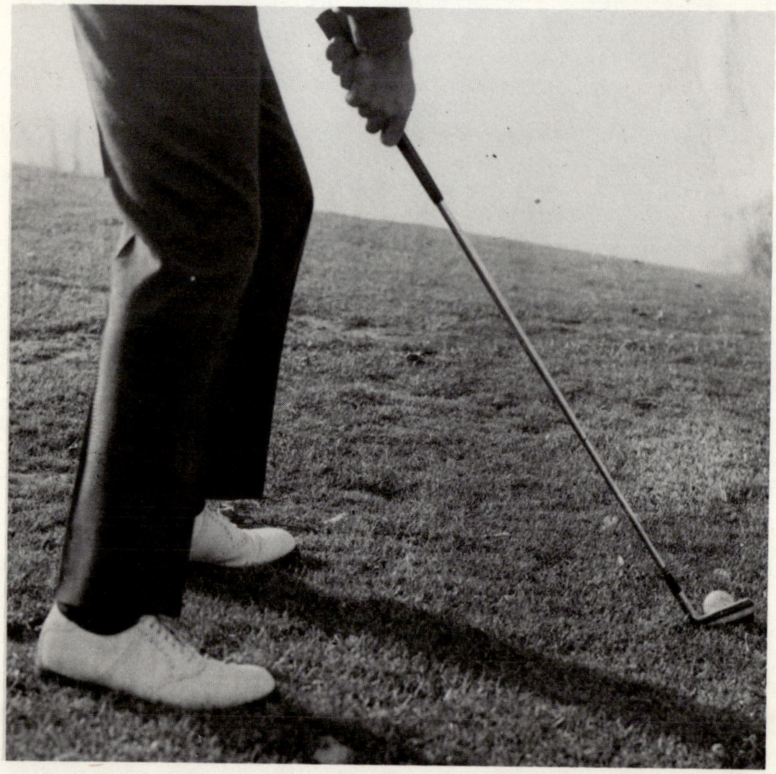

Downhill

Downhill lies are the most difficult of the uneven situations. Play the ball back in the stance, using the steepness of the slope as a guide to actual placement. The steeper the slope, the farther back in the stance the ball should be. Level yourself by bending the uphill leg. Use one more number club than usual (a 4-iron rather than a 3-iron) because the lower trajectory that results from this lie will make up for the loss of distance. Set your hands ahead and allow for a fade equal to the slope. When you swing, make sure that you follow the contour of the land. Take the club back up the hill and extend the club down the hill on the follow-through. Don't try to lift the ball with your hands or you'll come off the shot and top it.

Uphill

Flex the uphill knee to achieve balance and use a less-lofted club (a 3-iron instead of a 4-iron). Place the ball about midway in the stance with the hands ahead. Plan on a hook equal to the slope. When you swing, make sure the takeaway goes down the hill rather than straight up from the ball. The biggest problem the average golfer has here is that he tends to pick up the club with his hands. With the uphill leg flexed, you've created a level lie and the club is taken back along the ground on level lies until it rises of its own accord.

(Top left) Ball above feet: Stand farther away, choke down on the club, weight on balls of feet to create level lie.
(Top right) Downhill: Ball played to rear of stance, right leg bent, hands set ahead.
(Bottom) Uphill: Left leg flexed, ball at middle of stance.

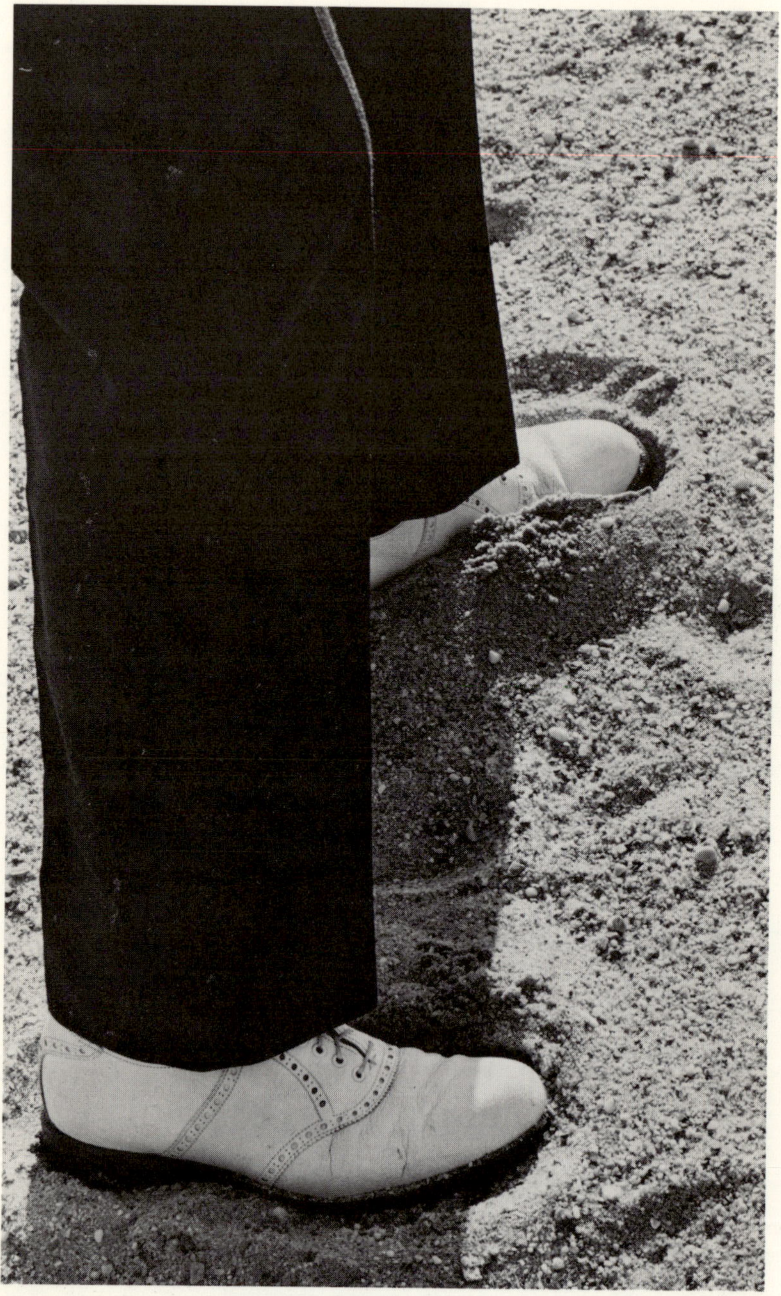

In the Sand

Fairway Traps

The first thing to remember about this shot is the first word—fairway. Just as you would from the fairway, you must strike the ball first, not the sand. As an aid, you might try looking at the front, rather than the back, of the ball. It is better to hit this shot thin than to catch the sand behind the ball.

    A little extra time should be spent in setting up to hit this shot. Since sand is loose, you've got to dig in to keep yourself from slipping. This is easily achieved by rotating the feet. The ball is played a little forward of center, and your weight is centered on your left side. You're not allowed the privilege of grounding your club, so take extra care to stay relaxed instead of stiffly holding the club above the ball. This stiffness is tension, and tension will ruin any shot.

    On the backswing, avoid any excessive transfer of weight to the right side. Keep the left knee pointed at the ball, not behind the ball. However, make a full turn with the upper body just as you would from the fairway.

    The move back to the ball is exactly the same as you use for all shots, with the hands remaining cocked and the left side leading. The ball gets hit first and the club continues on, taking a small sand divot. You can hit the ball as far from a fairway trap as you can from the fairway, but it might be a good idea to take a less-lofted club and swing easier, just as another way to avoid lunging.

    By the way, always rake your footprints smooth after you hit your shot so the next player doesn't land in one and have an extra-difficult shot.

For firm footing in the sand, wiggle your feet until you're anchored.

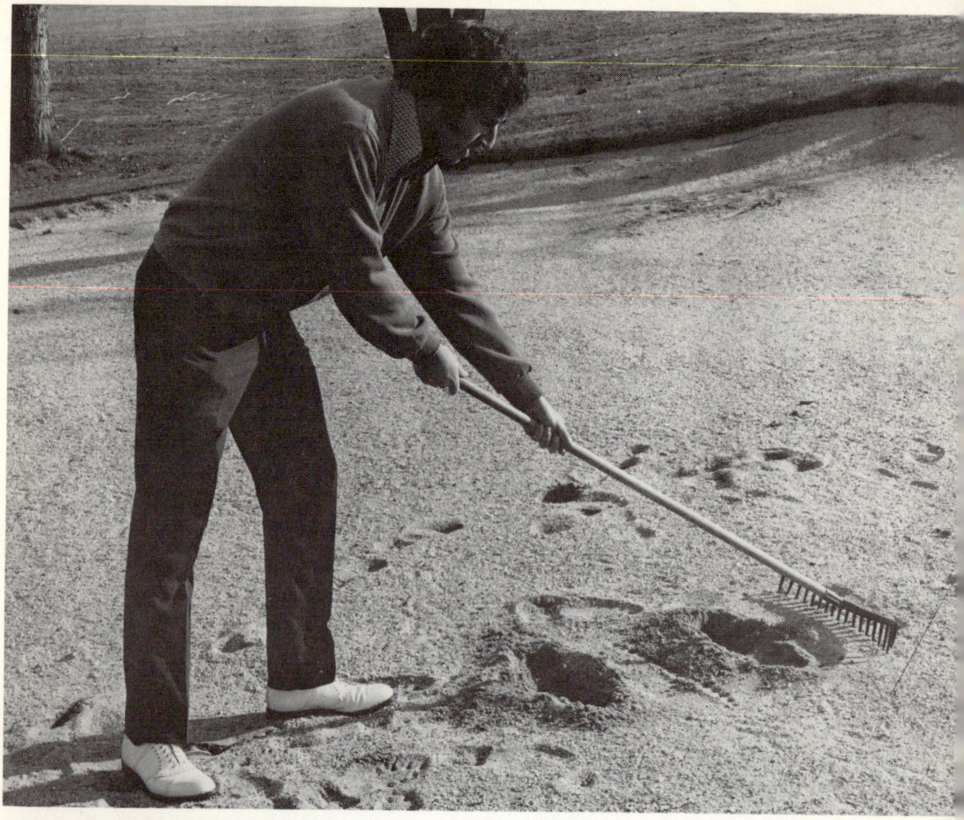

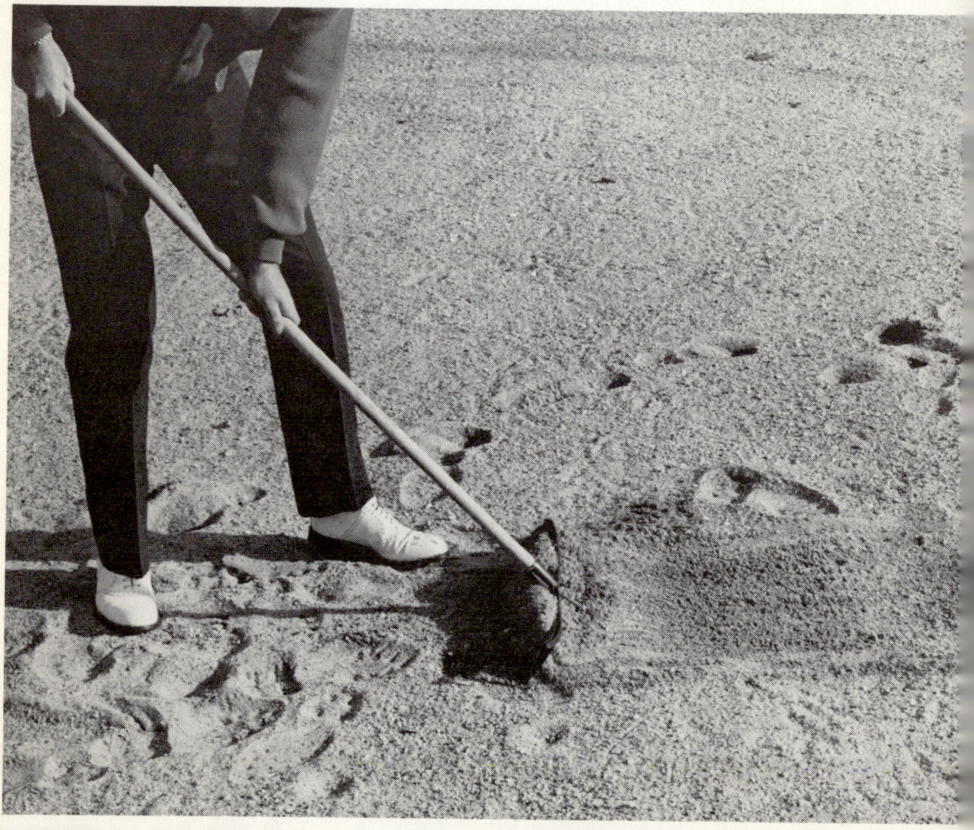

The Greenside Bunker

The greenside bunker is the only shot in golf that requires you NOT hit the ball. When you're faced with this type of shot, you've obviously got to have a completely different approach. If you don't want to hit the ball, what do you want to hit? The average player thinks "blast" and pounds down on the sand with his teeth gritted and his body rigid.

Actually, the stroke should be made with a minimum of effort under normal conditions. All you have to do is slide the club directly under the ball and follow-through. To get backspin and to prevent digging, you want to cut across the line of flight with the clubface rather than try to throw the club directly at the flag as you would on a fairway shot. There's a good reason for this: your swing is grooved to hit the ball when you line up at the target. You'd have to force it out of its groove in order to hit the sand shot, and in golf you don't want to "force" anything.

You set up with the left side facing on a forty-five-degree angle to the left of the target. The hands are well ahead of the face of the sand wedge, which lies almost flat. Place your weight almost exclusively on your left side. Now your swing can follow your body line just as it does on any other shot. The extremely open face of the wedge and the fact that you don't hit the ball will compensate for your body aim. The club slides directly under the ball (entering the sand at a point about two inches behind the ball) and the sand is thrown into the ball, driving it out at an angle from your body toward the target. If the sand is hard, cut down on the angle you aim your body to the left and close the face of the wedge by an equal amount.

Always rake your footprints smooth when you leave a trap so that the next player doesn't have to play out of a hole left by your shoes.

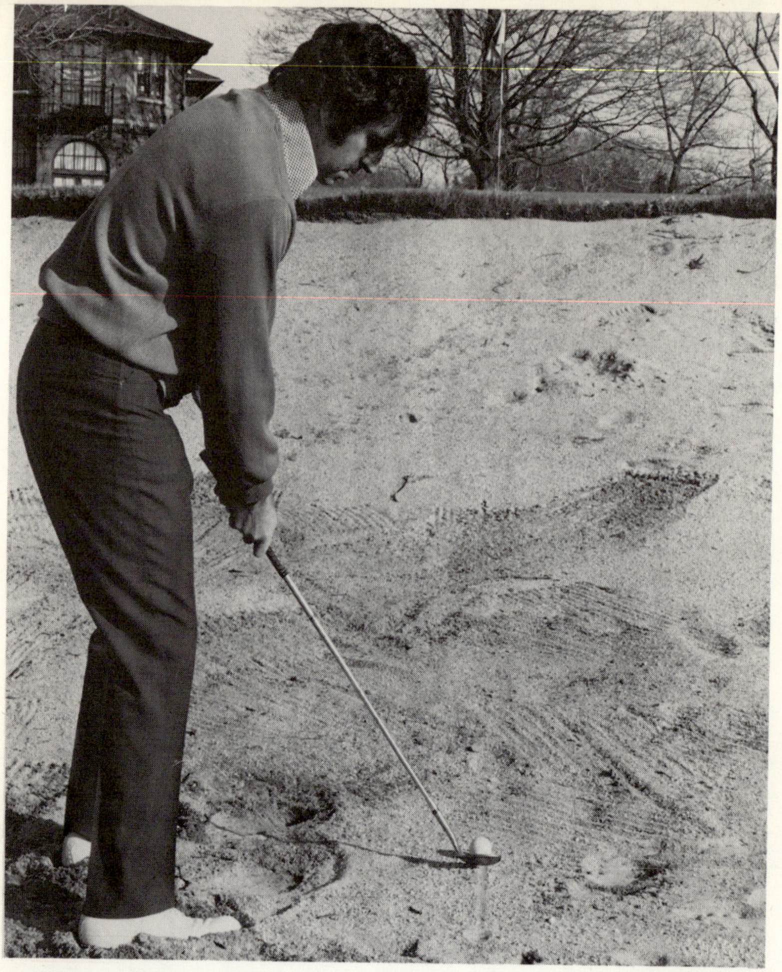

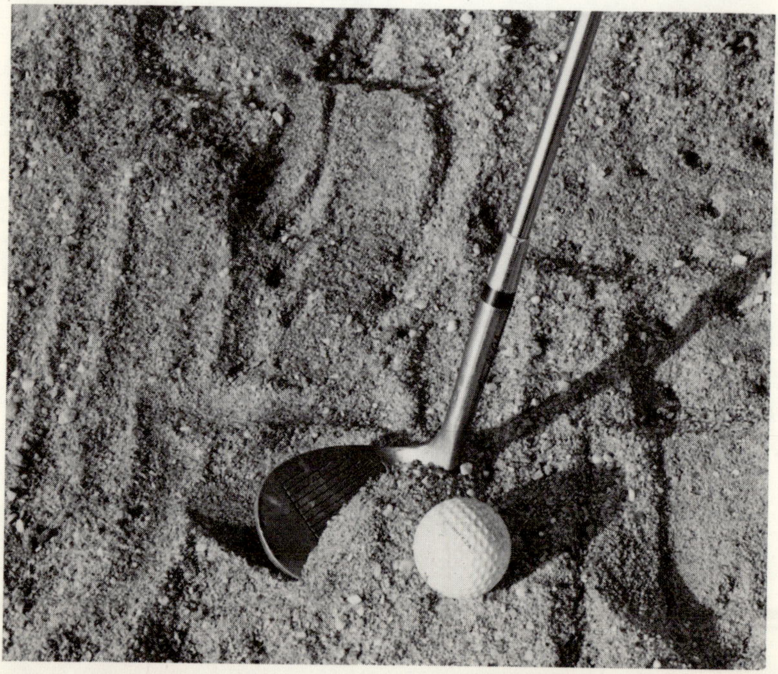

The stroke is made more with the arms than the hands in order to ensure the sliding action. When the hands do most of the work, the club tends to dig. With a little practice, you'll find this shot to be actually rather easy.

Address the ball with your body angled to the left of the flag and plan on cutting under the ball and across the line.

Enter the sand about two inches behind the ball with the club face open.

Section Four: Putting

How to Read a Green

Perhaps the great beauty of golf is its combination of mind, strength, and delicacy. The inch tap-in counts the same on the scorecard as the lag that got it there, the same as the iron shot that guided the ball to the green, and the same as the long drive that put the ball on the fairway. To play well, you need master only one aspect of the game, whether it be the long game or the short game. But to be a champion, you have to combine the two.

The great drivers, the ones who place their emphasis on hitting the ball 240 yards or more, tend to ignore their putting. But every tournament is won by the golfer with the hot putter, the one who's getting the ball in the hole.

To putt well, you have to understand the subtleties of grain, moisture, and contour that exist in every green, since each affects the way the ball will roll after it is hit.

Grain

As you walk up to a green from the fairway, notice its sheen. If the grass is dull, the grain is running toward you. If it is shiny, the grain is growing away from you. Thus, if the grass looks dull and your ball is short of the pin, you'll be putting against the

Remember that the grain grows away from mountains and toward water. Look for overhanging grass at the cup to discover the direction of the grain.

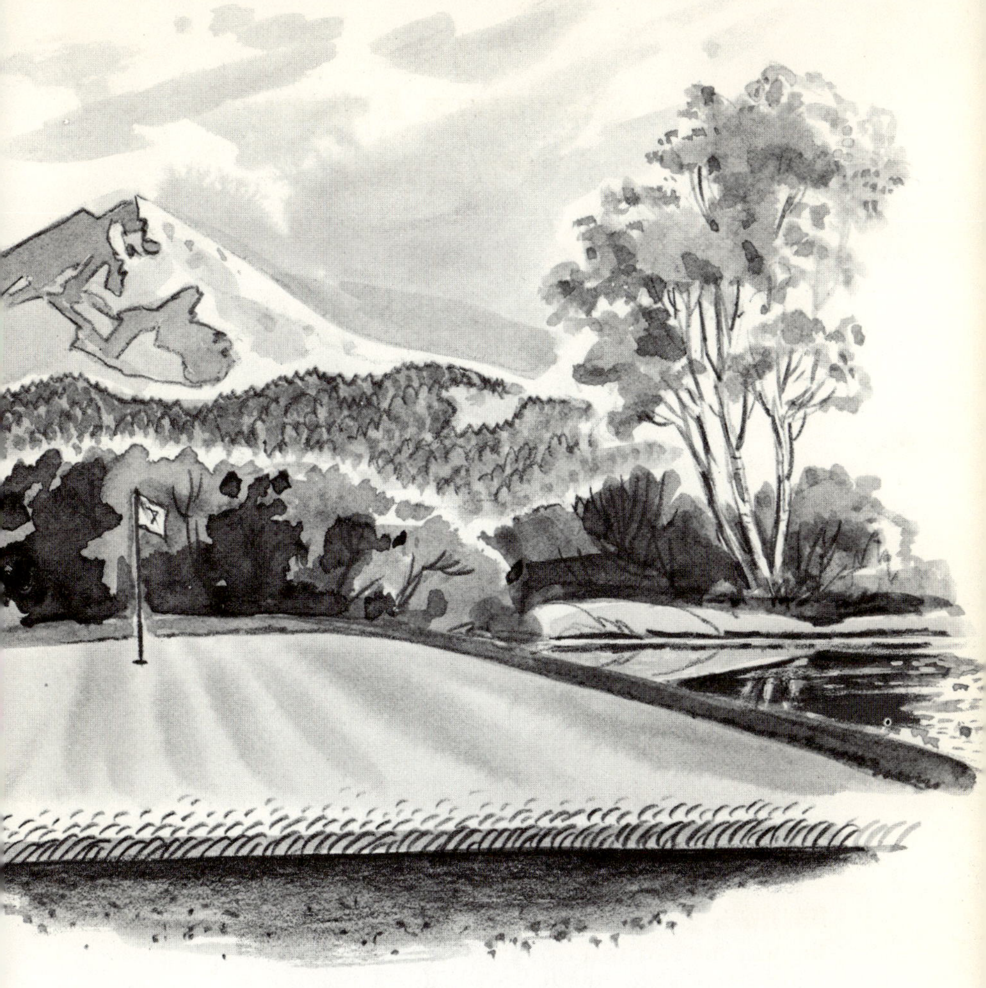

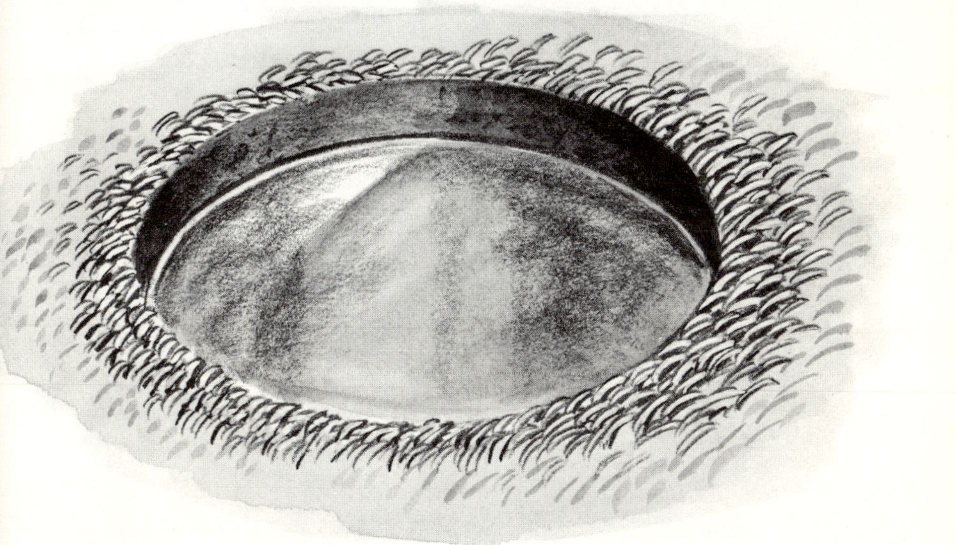

grain. When putting against the grain, you've got to hit the putt as though it were longer than it is, about a foot longer for every six feet of putt. So if you've got a thirty-foot putt against the grain, you should figure it to be a thirty-six-footer. Just the opposite is true if you're putting with the grain. Since the grass is growing in the same direction in which you're putting, it will help the ball keep the original speed that you imparted to it with your stroke. A thirty-foot putt thus becomes a twenty-four-footer on a level surface.

Grain will generally run in the direction in which a green slopes. But you should be careful around water, because the grass will probably grow toward the water even if it is in the opposite direction of the slope. If you're playing on a course near the mountains, the grain almost always grows away from the mountains.

As a last check, look at the grass at the edge of the cup. The grass will overhang on the side corresponding to the direction in which the grass is growing; the mower will clip the grass short on the other side.

Moisture

If the green is wet, the ball will slide across the surface because the blades won't have a chance to grab the ball and impede its roll to any great extent. On a wet green, a breaking putt will turn only about half as much as it would on a dry day. On straight putts, the water will have a greater effect on putts against the grain than it will on putts with the grain. Don't forget that you are allowed to lift your ball from casual water, even on the green.

Figuring the break of the putt should be an instinct call. Aim for the point at which the ball will turn toward the cup rather than at the cup itself.

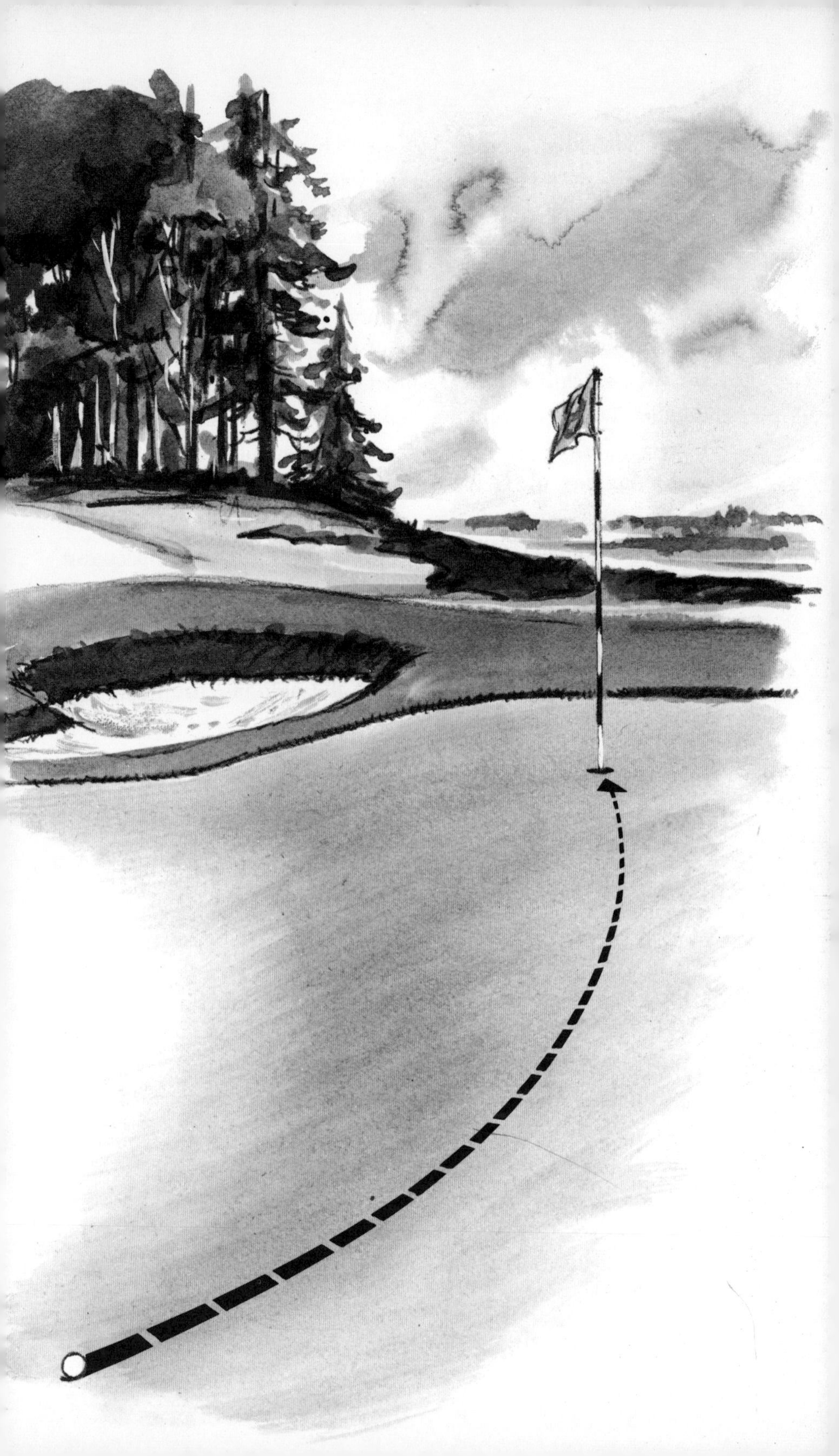

Incidentally, a green that hasn't been cut should be treated in the same way as one that is wet when you read it.

Contour

You should decide one thing right at the start—there is no way short of mechanizing your swing and using a protractor to be sure of a sidehill putt. It is something that you can spend twenty minutes looking at from twelve different angles and all you'll do, if you're lucky, is confirm what your eyes told you in the first place. Judging where the ball will break is an instinct call, so go directly to your first impression. Hit the ball at the point where you think the ball will start falling off the slope down toward the cup, not at the cup itself.

On uphill putts, you've got to hit the putt a little firmer, so aim for the back of the cup.

On downhill putts, try to have the ball just drop over the front lip of the cup.

Stance and Stroke

Planning a Putt

After you've figured out the grain and any other factors that might affect the roll and speed of the putt, you've got to see the "line" it is going to travel along. This line, from the ball to the cup, is the guide for the stroke and prevents the hands from trying to "steer" the putt. Developing this clear mental picture of the ball's path is essential if you hope to become a great putter. You've got to see the ball going in before you knock it in.

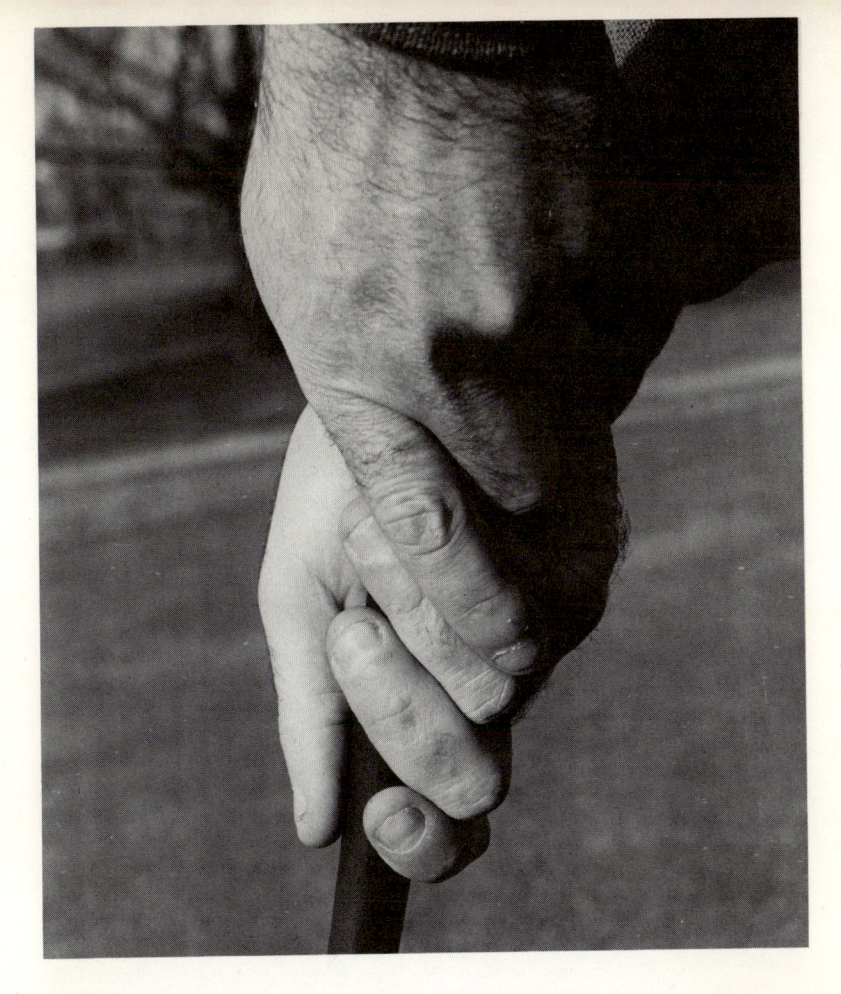

The popular reverse overlap grip used for putting — the forefinger of your left hand overlaps the fingers of the right hand giving more unity to the hands.

Grip

It is not imperative that you use the popular reverse overlap grip, but most pros feel it better unifies the hands and lets the right hand guide the club down the mental line once the ball has been struck. In this grip the index finger of the left hand overlaps the fingers of the right hand. The club is cradled in the middle pads of the fingers and is held gently but solidly.

Stance is optional in putting, but the head should be directly over the ball and the position of the rest of your body comfortable.

Stance

The body really isn't important in the act of putting, so its position should be comfortable and arranged to allow free action of the hands. Stand any way that you like, but make sure that you don't move as you putt. The best way to stand is the way that gives you the best perspective of the hole. To this end, get your eyes directly over the ball. If the ball is too far from the feet, it is difficult for the body to stay locked in comfortably. If you're

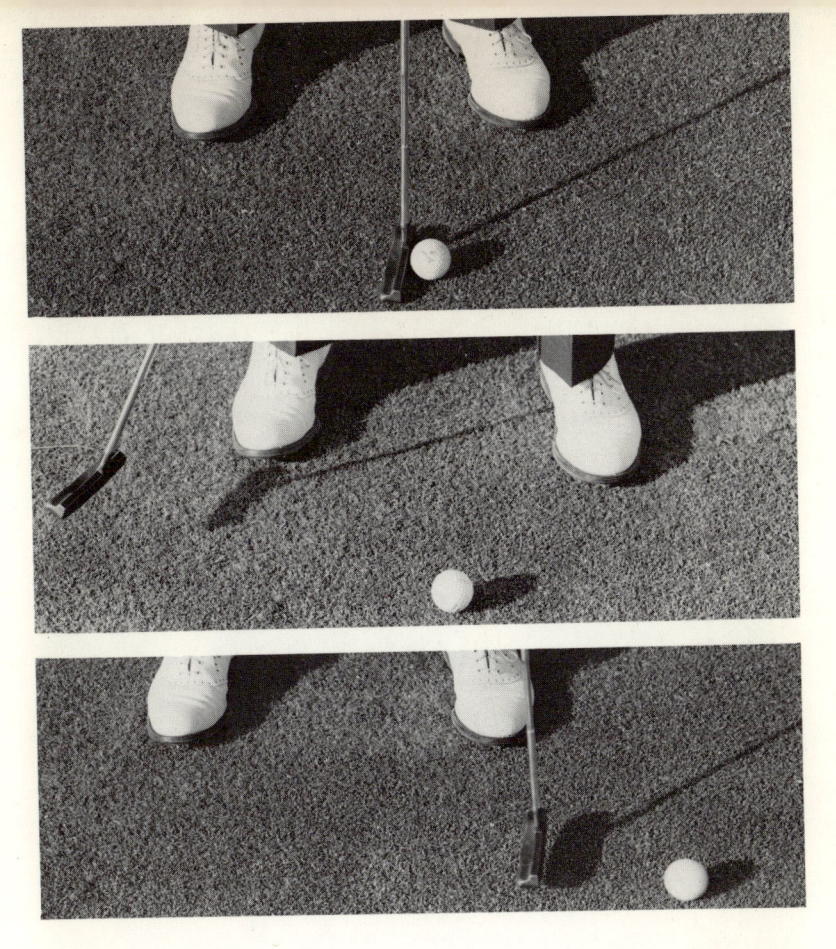

The Putting Stroke: A low, pendulum movement with no thought of stopping the club at any point. Let it go back as far as it wants to, then let it swing back through the ball toward the cup.

right-eye dominated, play the ball off the left foot with your head turned slightly toward the hole. If you're left-eye dominated, position the ball in the center of your stance and turn your head slightly toward your right foot.

Stroke

The stroke is a low pendulum movement. The club swings freely toward the cup, with the right hand dominating the follow-through. You should think of it as an underhand throw, letting the palm of the right hand extend straight at the hole.

Start the stroke with a small forward press of the hands and then let it swing back low along the ground. The club should be allowed to go back as far as it wants to, then released to go forward. The club will pull the hands toward impact, forcing the right hand to take over the stroke as contact is made with the ball.

Section Five:
The Proper State of Mind

Relaxation

Relax

Tension breeds tightness, and tight muscles are immobile muscles. Tension goes beyond the physical, too, and can destroy feelings, awareness, concentration, and composure. It is, therefore, imperative to be as relaxed as you possibly can when you swing a golf club, so that you can be in command of your body and be aware of what's happening to it at every moment in the swing. The closer you come to that kind of awareness, the better golfer you will be.

Most players will tighten just as they start their swing and turn the swing into a backward and forward motion that changes every time it happens. They wind up hitting the ball in a state of fear, more worried about where the ball is going to land than they are about how they're going to get it where they want it to go.

Some Tips on Avoiding Tension

Always remember that the ball has no power to move by itself; it can only be moved by the action of the club. It only goes where it's told to go by the speed and path of the club at impact. As long as you control the club, you control the ball.

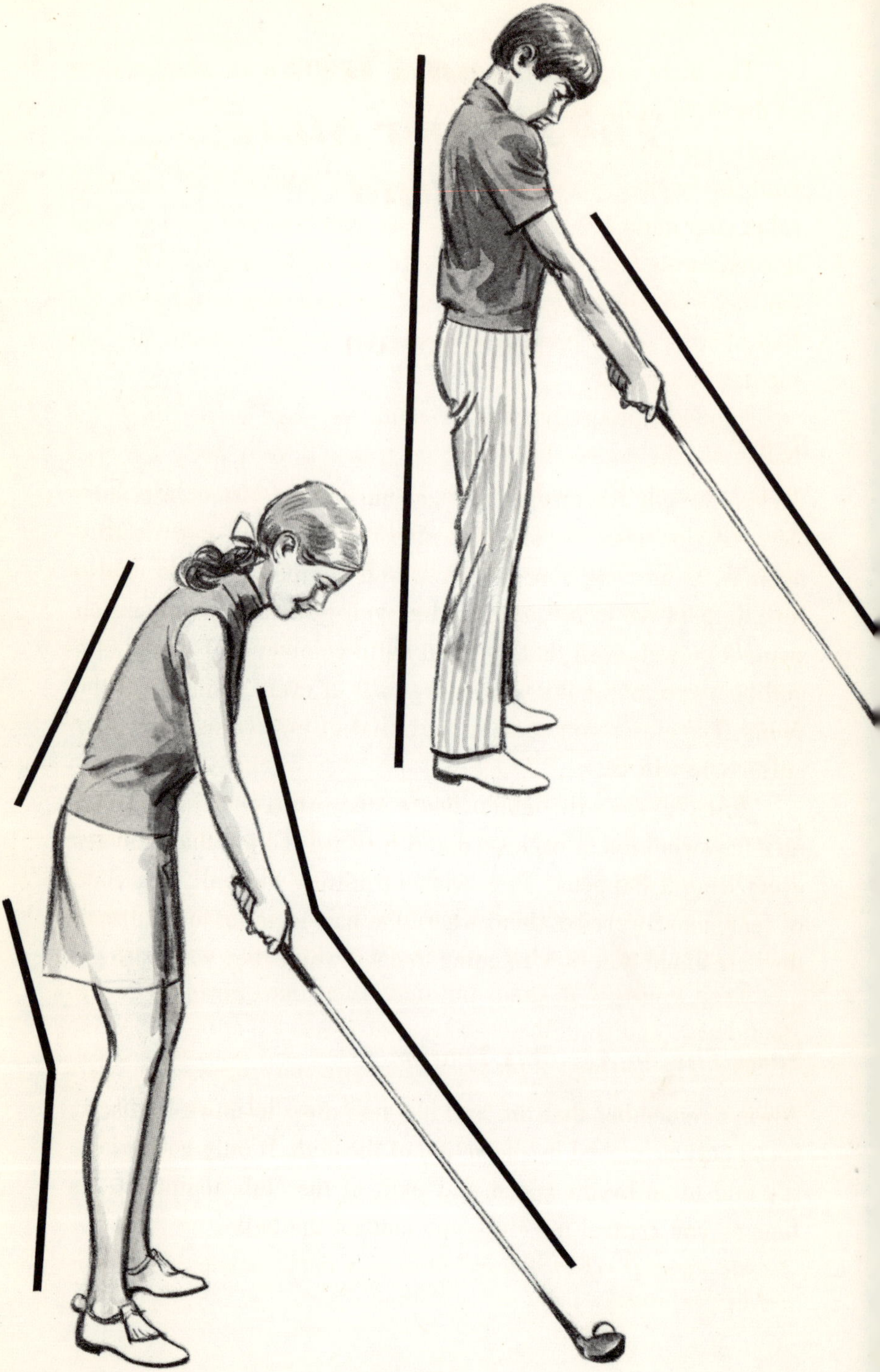

The flight of the ball is nothing more than an exaggeration of the flight of the clubhead.

If you have trouble avoiding tension, try relaxing parts of your body that demonstrate tension to others. For instance, relax your mouth. When you're tense, your lips will tighten. That tension in the mouth reflects the attitude of the entire body. You can help yourself relax simply by smiling as you address the ball. You'll notice immediately the difference it makes in your mental awareness.

Another important tension point is your grip. Since the hands are the connecting rods that transmit your body's energy to the club, tension will "freeze" your energy source and leave you with a weak hitting action. Make sure you grip the club in the fingers and that you feel as though the fingers are in control of the swinging action of the club.

Don't just keep your eye on the ball. Try to see the path along which you want the clubhead to be traveling as it moves through the ball. The club acts just like your hands; it will go where your eyes tell it to go.

Waggle the club slightly before you swing, and when you're ready to start the swing, use a small forward press of the hands to break the last bit of tension that might exist.

Take a couple of deep breaths while you plan the shot; you'll get a better image of what you'll need to do when you swing.

Keep yourself in good physical condition. Strength breeds confidence, and confidence eliminates fear.

Don't be anxious to hit the ball as you're swinging. The right hand will release itself at the bottom of the club's arc.

A tense stance is reflected everywhere, even in the mouth. Smile, relax, and be comfortable.

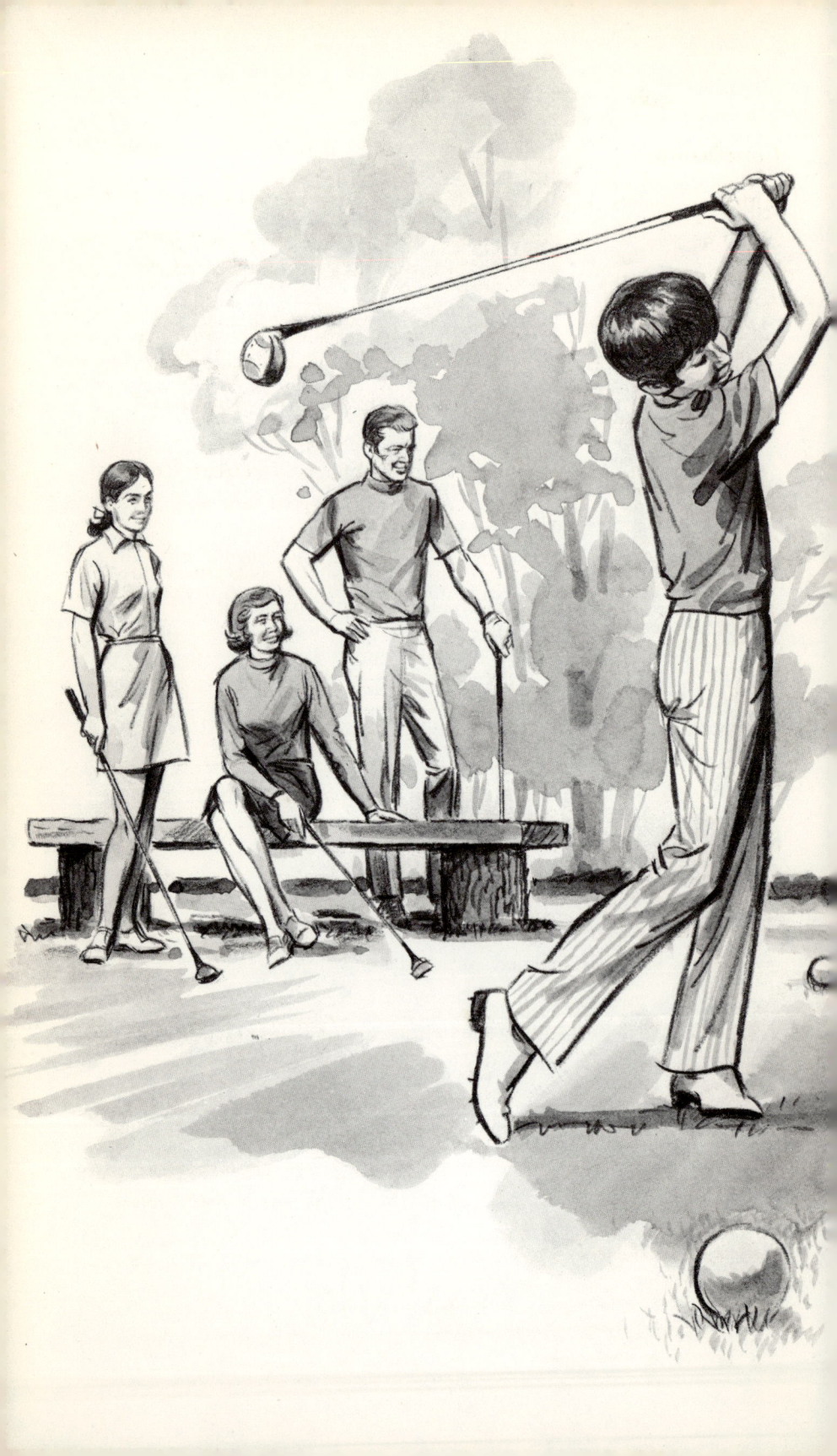

Conclusion

Although society has taught us that results are important, it might be wise to consider that golf is primarily an escape from society into a world of great beauty where enjoyment can be found at all levels of ability.

In every round, you're sure to hit two or three shots that are essentially beyond your capability. The thrill you derive from these shots will bring you back again to the golf course, and you'll hit those two or three sweet ones again.

Use golf as a discovery of your body, as a retreat from stress, and as a source of joy, and it will reward you with all this and more.

Approach the game of golf and every shot it contains with anticipation rather than determination—and approach it with the whole family. You'll love it!

Golf is an ideal family game.

Glossary

Ace — A hole-in-one or making a score of one (1) on any hole.

Address — The position assumed by the player in preparation for hitting the ball.

Backswing — The complete movement of the club away from the ball.

Birdie — A score of one less than par on a hole (a 3 on a par 4 hole).

Bogey — A score of one more than par on a hole (a 5 on a par 4 hole).

Caddy — The person who carries the golfer's clubs.

Chip — A short shot made from just off the edge of the green.

Clubface — The part of the club that strikes the ball.

Dogleg — A hole that is designed with a bend in the middle of it.

Double Bogey — A score of two more than par on a hole (a 6 on a par 4 hole).

Downswing — The act of returning the club to the ball after the backswing.

Drive — A shot taken from the tee on a hole.

Eagle — A score of two less than par on a hole (a 2 on a par 4 hole).

Fairway — The finely manicured grass extending from the tee to the green.

"Fat" Hit — One in which the club contacts the ground before hitting the ball.

Follow-through — The finish of the swing after impact.

Green — The extremely low-cut area of grass on which the hole is located.

Honors — The method of determining the order of play from the tee.

Hook — A ball that has a flight path from right-to-left for right-handers and left-to-right for left-handers.

Impact — The actual moment the club hits the ball.

Making the Turn — Completing nine holes or half the course.

Match Play — Competition based on each hole in which the winner is the one scoring lower than his opponent on the majority of holes.

Medal or Stroke Play — A competition in which the winner is the player who hits the ball the fewest number of times during the round.

Out-of-Bounds — Beyond the confines of the course as defined by white stakes marked "OB."

Par — What a PROFESSIONAL is supposed to score on a hole based on the length of the hole. A par 3 hole can be as long as 250 yards, a par 4 hole is between 251 and 470 yards long, a par 5 is anything over 470 yards.

Pin — The flagstick that marks the location of the hole on the green.

Putt — A stroke made with a putter on the green.

Rough — The uncut grass bordering both sides of the fairway.

Round — Playing all eighteen holes of the golf course.

Shank — A shot that strikes the clubface at the point where it meets the shaft of the club, forcing the ball to go straight to the right (left for left-handers).

Skied Shot — A ball hit excessively high, resulting in a loss of distance.

"Skulled" Shot — Where the club strikes only the top half of the ball and sends it away on a low line drive.

Slice — The opposite of a hook, a path from left-to-right for right-handers.

Takeaway — The beginning of the swing when the club is moved away from the ball.

Tee — The marked-off area where play begins on each hole.

"Topped" Shot — Where the top of the ball is hit, causing it to roll along the ground rather than rise in the air.

Bibliography

Cromie, Robert A. *Golf for Boys and Girls*. Chicago: Follett, 1965.

Daro, August and Graffis, Herb. *Inside Swing: A Modern Technique for Better Golf*. New York: Thomas Y. Crowell, 1972.

Murphy, Michael. *Golf and the Kingdom*. New York: Viking Press, 1972.

Naden, Corinne J. *The First Book of Golf*. New York: Franklin Watts, 1970.

Nichols, Bobby. *Never Say Never*. New York: Fleet, 1965.

Sullivan, George. *The Champion's Guide to Golf*. New York: Fleet, 1966.

Index

Accuracy. *See* Control
Ace, defined, 56
Address, 6, 21, 26
    defined, 56
Alignment, 18-21. *See also* Perspective

Backswing, 14, 22-27, 31
    defined, 56
    left hand controls, 6
    position at top, 25-27
    in sand, 37
Balance:
    on backswing, 25
    on sloping ground, 32
Ball:
    controlled by club, 51-53
    on hillside, 32-35
    position relative to golfer, 13-14, 17, 18, 48-49
Baseball grip, 9, 11-13
Beginner:
    choice of clubs, 2
    mastery of grip, 9
Birdie, defined, 56
Bogey, defined, 56

Caddy, defined, 56

Championship play, 42
Chip, defined, 56
Club(s), 2-5
    aid in positioning, 18-20
    for beginners, 2
    choice on hillside, 35
    choice in sand, 37
    criteria for purchase, 2-3
    as extension of arm, 22, 53
    should suit body type, 3, 4, 5
Clubface, defined, 56
Clubhead, 3, 6
Contour, effect on putting, 46
Control, 6, 11, 51

Distance, variation in clubs, 2
Divot, 37
Dogleg, defined, 56
Double bogey, defined, 56
Downswing, 21, 27-28
    defined, 56
    left hand controls, 6
    in sand, 37
Drive, defined, 56
Driver, 2, 3, 5
    position on backswing, 25

Eagle, defined, 56

8 iron, 2
Errors, 9
Eye dominance in putting, 49
Fade, 14
    on hillside, 32
Fairway, 21
    defined, 56
"Fat" hit, 3
    defined, 56
5 iron, 2, 3
Follow-through, 28-31
    defined, 57

Girls, choice of clubs, 5
Golf:
    natural and logical, 13, 39
    source of joy, 53-55
Golf course, 21
Golf pro, 3
Golfer, influence of body build:
    on choice of clubs, 3, 4, 5
    on stance, 13, 14, 17
Grass, 42-46
Green, 2, 42-46
    defined, 57
    grain, 42-44
Greenside bunker, 39-41
Grip, 6, 9-13
    avoidance of tension, 53
    interlocking, 9, 11, 13
    need to check regularly, 9
    reverse overlap, 47
    ten-finger or baseball, 9, 11-13
    Vardon, 9, 11, 13
Grip size, 5, 11

Hand action, 5
    importance of unity, 9, 11-13
    only connection with club, 6
Hole, 18
Honors, defined, 57
Hook, 3, 11, 14, 17, 18
    defined, 57
    on hillside, 32

Impact, 6, 17, 28, 51
    defined, 57
Interlocking grip, 9, 11, 13
Irons, 2
    choice on hillside, 35
    position on back swing, 25

Landing area, 21
Left hand, test for grip, 13
Left side dominance, 6, 11, 22, 28

Making the turn, defined, 57
Match play, defined, 57
Medal play, defined, 57
Moisture on green, 44

Nicklaus, Jack, 11
9 iron, 2, 3

1 wood, 2
Out-of-bounds, defined, 57
Overswing, 21
Overturn, 14

Par, defined, 57
Parallel stance, 13-14
Perspective, 14, 17, 18
    in putting, 46, 48
Pin, defined, 57
Power, 6
Problems:
    carelessness, 9

clubs as aid in correction, 3, 4, 5
Putt, defined, 57
Putter, 2
Putting, 42-50
    green, 42-46
    grip, 47
    instinct, 46
    stance, 48-49
    stroke, 49-50

Relaxation, 13, 15, 28, 37, 51-53. *See also* Tension
Right hand:
    controls impact, 6, 28
    guides putt, 47, 50
Rough, defined, 57
Round, defined, 57

Sand trap, 2, 37-41
    Fairway traps, 37
Sand wedge, 2, 39
7 iron, 2
Shaft flex, 3-4, 5
Shank, defined, 57
Shots, 2, 13, 14
    all equal, 42
    defined, 57-58
    planning, 21
Skied shot, defined, 57
"Skulled" shot, defined, 57
Slice, 3, 14
    defined, 58
Speed, 3, 17, 51
Square stance, 13-14

Stance, 13-18
    closed, 14-18
    distance from ball, 18-21
    open, 14
    in putting, 48-49
    in sand, 37, 39
    square, 13-14
    for uneven lies, 32-35
Stroke, 49-50
Stroke play, defined, 57
Swing, 18, 21, 22-31, 51, 53
    on sand shot, 39
    on sloping ground, 32-35
Swing weight of clubs, 3-4, 5

Takeaway, 22
    defined, 58
Tee, defined, 58
Ten-finger grip, 9, 11-13
Tension, 6, 9, 13, 14
    how to avoid, 51-53
    inhibits natural motion, 22, 28, 37
3 iron, 2
3 wood, 2
"Topped" shot, defined, 58

Uneven lies, 32-35

Vardon grip, 9, 11, 13

Weight of clubs, 3-4
Wildness, 4, 5
Woods, 2
Women, choice of clubs, 5

ABOUT THE AUTHOR

PARKER SMITH was born in Brooklyn, New York, where he presently lives with his wife Sheila and their two cats. He received a B.A. degree from Memphis State University and studied television writing at the New School for Social Research. While working on news and special programs for the U.S. Army Signal Center Television Network, he was awarded ten official commendations by the U.S. Army. He later became a golf professional at Sunrise Acres Golf Club in Dexter, Maine. Mr. Smith is now Staff Instruction Editor for *Golf Magazine* and in his spare time he paints. He is also the president of the Rainy Day Fun Company which designs educational games and toys, including *Rainy Day Golf*, the first instructional golf game.

DICKINSON MIDDLE SCHOOL LIBRARY

9435

DICKINSON MIDDLE SCHOOL LIBRARY.

796.352 Smith, Parker
Smi
        Golf techniques

DATE DUE	BORROWER'S NAME	ROOM NUMBER
FEB 23 '77	M. Sikorski	224
MAY 11 '78	Russell Lechtanski	
APR 12 '78	Jeff Lazuka	201
NOV 29		

796.352 Smith, Parker
Smi
        Golf techniques